introduces a pragmatic framework for how those practices must evolve to compete and win in today's environment. Definitely a must-read for leaders of any-sized organization or team."

—Brad D. Smith, President and CEO, Intuit

"Prasad unearths a fundamental truth posited by Darwin and connects it to business—namely, that agility and emotional intelligence are as vital to business as they are to human survival. If we want to compete to win in the jungle of business, we must gear up as emotionally intelligent and human-centered leaders of dynamic cultures that enable the realization of a strategically agile business model. This is a powerful articulation of a new axiom that will define business strategy in the decades to come."

—John Replogle,
CEO, Seventh Generation

"The one thing you need to understand to win in business today? *Nimble*. Do it, be it, and strive for it. Baba Prasad's latest book will show you how."

—Claire Díaz-Ortiz,
early Twitter employee and Silicon Valley innovator

"Baba Prasad drives the point that just having smart people is not enough for companies' success; rather, a company culture that enables people to apply different intelligences will make them into agile entrepreneurs and empowered change agents, and give greater success to the company over competitors. Very true indeed."

—Frans van Houten, CEO, Royal Philips NV

"In a world where turmoil is the only constant, *Nimble* charts a bold new path for leadership, strategy, and innovation. This is a mindset-changing book for executives and students of business."

—Don Tapscott, bestselling author of
The Digital Economy: Rethinking Promise and Peril in the Age of Networked Intelligence (Anniversary Edition)

"Baba Prasad's breaking up of strategic agility into five distinct components that are applicable to both strategic development and execution will make this an extremely useful tool for strategy practitioners. Visionary agility needs to go hand in hand with operational agility."

—Jyoti Narang, former COO, Luxury Division, Taj Hotels

Nimble

*Make Yourself and Your
Company Resilient in the
Age of Constant Change*

Baba Prasad

A TarcherPerigee Book

tarcherperigee

An imprint of Penguin Random House LLC
375 Hudson Street
New York, New York 10014

First published in India by Random House India 2015
This revised edition with a new introduction published 2018

Most TarcherPerigee books are available at special quantity
discounts for bulk purchase for sales promotions, premiums,
fund-raising, and educational needs. Special books or book
excerpts also can be created to fit specific needs. For details,
write: SpecialMarkets@penguinrandomhouse.com.

ISBN 9780143131458 (hc.)
ISBN 9781524705183 (ebook)

Printed in the United States of America
1   3   5   7   9   10   8   6   4   2

Book design by Katy Riegel

Contents

//

Introduction

I F YOU ARE the CEO of a company—start-up to Fortune 100—you know that change, rapid change, is staring you in the face. The business world is described so often today by words like "turbulent," "volatile," "uncertain," "unpredictable," "chaotic," and "ambiguous." To complicate matters, not only is change inevitable, but it is also happening at an ever-increasing speed and with unprecedented impact. As a CEO, you know firsthand that coping with change has become an issue of survival. Adaptation seems to be a likely response in this situation. And adaptation as a means to handle change has been around from the time of Charles

We can no longer afford to adapt slowly.

Darwin. But there's a problem. We can no longer afford to adapt slowly, at evolutionary rates. We need to be able to change rapidly. We need agility in our business.

So it's not surprising that when PricewaterhouseCoopers asked 1,400 CEOs to name the one capability that would be most critical for their companies to develop, the majority answered "business agility." Similarly, 400 CEOs surveyed by KPMG's *US CEO Outlook 2016* placed an unprecedented emphasis on business agility. The trend is not new. In 2009, the Economist Intelligence Unit conducted a similar survey—it interviewed 349 business executives in nineteen different industries across eight countries. It found that for an overwhelming majority of executives (88 percent), organizational agility is key to global success. And, most strikingly, for 50 percent of all CEOs and CIOs, agility not only is important but is a "core differentiator." An MIT study suggests that agility is connected to profits: agile firms grow revenue 37 percent faster and generate 30 percent higher profits than nonagile companies.[1] Clearly, it's a no-brainer: we have to be agile to survive and thrive.

But like CEOs across the world who clearly recognize the need for business agility, you are not alone if you're lying awake at night. All this talk about agility sounds great. But like the drunk who won't leave the bar, the question persists in the back of your mind: In these times of turbulent change—with lightning shifts in technology, unpredictable customers and labor, unending market disruptions, and unforeseeable competitors—*how* can I make and keep my company agile? *How* can I develop, in my people and in my company, the capacity to turn on a dime? To be light enough to move fast and also heavy enough to pack a punch? And if your company is big, you may further wonder, Can my giant company become at all nimble in the first place?

A second set of questions bothers you at a personal level: Do *I* have the agility to make decisions quickly when so many pieces of the puzzle are moving so fast? How can I show leadership in the midst of all this turbulence? How can I assess my agility as a leader, and what should I do to improve it?

In this book I'll show you how, even in the midst of chaotic change, you can take a set of steps to make your company and yourself become nimble. I'll show you how to build agility into your company culture—into the people, the processes, the mind-set, the works. You'll learn how to become nimble, not only in your leadership at work, but also in your personal capacity, at home and in your community. You'll also learn to think differently about agility itself. You will see that there is not one kind but five different kinds of agilities that you and your company need to build and apply in a way that is most fitting to your context. And, most important, you'll learn how necessary it is to build long-term responses, even though you might be tempted to react solely in the short term. In other words, you will learn how to make yourself and your company *strategically agile.*

Background

The idea that drives this book goes back to 1997, when the e-commerce boom, riding on the newly available Internet, was rocking the world—a time when exciting new business models and paradigms were being at once constructed and challenged. Like many other business strategists in the late 1990s, I realized that companies need to be adaptable, flexible, and agile in order to cope with uncertainty—that is by no means a dramatic insight, and of course one need not be a rocket scientist to come to that conclusion. However, the question still remains: *How?* What specific steps do we need to take to become agile leaders and create nimble companies?

Over the last hundred years, since Frederick Winslow Taylor wrote his seminal book *The Principles of Scientific Management* (1911), we have learned tremendously well how to manage organizations by optimizing the use of various kinds of resources. We know how to structure organizations for optimal flows of control, goods, and information. We have become adept in leveraging technologies for competitive advantage and in lean-and-mean methodologies. We have black-belt expertise in Six Sigma methods that lead to dramatic improvements in production quality. But since the 1990s, we have all come to recognize that the lessons in optimization and efficiency that we have gathered are not adequate in today's turbulent world. So should we throw all this out of the window? No. This knowledge and expertise is far from irrelevant today—in fact, it's essential for us to run profitable businesses. The case I'll be making in the chapters that follow is that principles of scientific management are necessary but are not sufficient to deal with a rapidly changing, uncertain, and unpredictable world. The Taylorian mind-set of the business executive and business organization has to be expanded to include a mind-set of agility. This book will show you how.

At the risk of sounding like a new age guru, let me tell you: the magic sauce to becoming a leader who makes quick decisions but is also strategic, the secret to creating an agile company that is also visionary, is *inside you*. Let me explain.

In 1999, I moved to a new faculty position at the Carlson School of Management at the University of Minnesota. This started me on a different track altogether—Carlson is a more behaviorally oriented school than the companies and universities where I had previously trained or worked. One evening I stepped back from all my economic models of markets, competition, firm structure—the kind of mumbo-jumbo that ruled my mind as a business school professor—and asked a simple question: How do we as individuals handle uncertainty in our daily life? We miss a flight to an important meeting, or the school calls in the middle of a busy workday to say our child is sick, and so on. What capability do we draw on when we are in an unfamiliar setting or faced with a sudden crisis?

Beginning with this set of questions, I began, over the next few weeks, to learn about an incredible system that has, over millions of years, demonstrated a tremendous ability to be agile. That system is within me and within you—it is the human system! Think about it. We are wired to be agile. When we face a new situation or have a new problem to solve, we piece together various things we know to create a new solution; when we don't know, we learn. What drives this improvisation, this learning? Our intelligence.

We are wired to be agile.

So, as a B-school professor, I began to focus on how a firm might create strategy using the concept of intelligence as a driver of agility. What is the equivalent of human intelligence in organizations? I asked. Can we measure it? Can we develop it? Over the last ten years, through my consulting practice, I have refined the concept into a framework that I call the Vivékin Intelligences Framework (VIF).[2] As I will show in subsequent chapters, you can use this tremendously practical system to develop into a leader with five different agilities—analytical, operational, inventive, communicative, and visionary—and also to build these five agilities into your company so it can respond dynamically to uncertainty and even thrive in it.

As you will recognize, the intelligence approach is a paradigm shift. It shakes us out of the comfort of a mind-set that sees companies as decision-making machines that use technologies to make business processes lean and mean. It pushes us toward a more comprehensive, humanist mind-set that sees the company as comprising inanimate processes and technologies but also living, thinking, and feeling people. The intelligence approach also breaks the artificial divide we have built between hard analytical models of strategy that attempt to make companies into industry leaders, and softer behavioral approaches that seek to develop individuals into leaders. It moves us from models of strategy focused on assessing and managing risk to strategic thinking geared to deal with uncertainty; it shifts our understanding of intelligence and agility from the singular to the plural, making us think of multiple intelligences and multiple agilities that we can apply depending on the context.

Above all, the intelligence approach to strategy and leadership reaffirms our faith in a human system that over millions of years has faced and overcome all kinds of challenges—some sudden and turbulent, others gradual and evolutionary. And because the intelligence approach taps into what makes us characteristically human and indeed gives our species its name—*homo sapiens*—a system for strategy and leadership based on a model of human intelligence is natural for us to interpret and easy for us to apply.

Agility from the Five-Intelligences Perspective

Anthropologists Nicholas Burbules and Paul Smeyers recount a story told to them by a woman who had been running a soup kitchen very successfully in Chicago.[3] Once, when she was a little girl, the woman had been helping her mother wash dishes. Accidentally, a cup slipped from her hand and smashed into pieces on the kitchen floor. Before she could even cry, her mother picked up another cup, threw it on the floor, and said, "See? It doesn't matter."

This is a simple story of everyday life. What does it illustrate, though? Most apparently, of course, as Burbules and Smeyers say, the story is about how a mother reassured her child that material things do not matter and that we all make mistakes, and about how, through a simple action, she conveyed that she was not angry. But at a deeper level, this story is a lesson in leadership: it shows how someone in greater authority handles a subordinate's mistake. Considering that the woman recounted the story sixty years later, it is clear that the experience formed a "lesson" in agile leadership that had stayed with her for decades.

I like this story because it sums up my approach to agility. From the perspective of the five-intelligences framework, to be agile means to be fast-moving in order to handle rapidly changing circumstances but, at the same time, to do it with a view to the long term. In other words, agility is about combining speed with long-term vision. Other approaches to agility that emphasize short-term speed over long-term vision are about tactics, not about strategy. Nimble leaders and companies use the five-intelligences approach to achieve lasting success through strategic agility.

Using the intelligences framework I present in this book, I have worked with leaders and companies across the world to help them understand, develop, and apply the five agilities they need to become resilient, transformational leaders and to make their companies both agile and visionary—no matter what comes their way.

As I will show you in later chapters, I have developed on the work of military strategists to build a very effective plan to use the five intelligences—I call it the MAST cycle. MAST is an acronym that stands for "mapping, assessing, strategizing, and testing." Using this method and the five-intelligences framework, I will show how you can:

- systematically evaluate what intelligences or agilities your current situation is demanding (map),
- determine your current resources and what you are lacking (assess),
- strategize about how you can use your resources or capabilities or develop them to handle the situation (strategize),
- and apply them in a small-scale test to enhance your effort if the test indicates success, or pivot if the test calls for a different approach (test).

As you adopt the five-intelligences framework and apply the MAST cycle, you will realize that you have a powerful tool that will enable you to lead in the most dynamically changing circumstances. And the best thing is that the process also makes you a better person in many ways.

Chapter 1

Strategy and Leadership in Turbulent Times

O<small>N</small> D<small>ECEMBER</small> 23, 2011, the Joint Typhoon Warning Center in Pearl Harbor, Hawaii, reported that a tropical disturbance had begun to form in the Indian Ocean, about nine hundred miles to the east of Indonesia. Over the next two days, the disturbance trekked northwest, with winds near its center reaching forty miles an hour. It was now strong enough to be classified as a tropical storm and about six hundred miles to the southeast of Chennai in India. Soon the India Meteorological Department recategorized it as a tropical depression and named it Depression BOB 05. Within the next forty-eight hours, Depression BOB 05 progressed successively—and quickly—first into a deep depression, then into a cyclonic storm, and after that into a very severe cyclonic storm with winds reaching speeds of more than one hundred miles an hour. By then it had also had acquired a name: Cyclone Thane. On December 30, 2011, Thane struck the southeastern coast of India with the force of a Category 1 hurricane.

EID Parry, one of India's major sugar producers, found its largest sugar factory, in Nellikuppam (in the south Indian state of Tamil Nadu), directly in the path of Cyclone Thane. By the time Thane passed, it had blown the roof off the Nellikuppam sugar factory and wreaked havoc on the production machinery. It was estimated that it would take the factory at least thirty days to become operational again. Thane had also destroyed four thousand acres of the sugarcane fields that supplied the factory. EID Parry had a gigantic problem on its hands— it had to crush and process ten thousand tons of sugarcane. There was a further complication. Sugarcane, once it is harvested, begins to lose its juice content rapidly— even a delay of twenty-four hours can cause considerable loss in cane weight because both moisture levels and the sucrose content of the juice decline dramatically. This short shelf life of harvested cane meant that EID Parry—with an inoperative factory—had no more than ten days to finish processing ten thousand tons of uprooted sugarcane.[4]

///////////

IT HAD BEEN a long day for Paul and Mary Zimby,[5] and after dinner they settled down on the couch of their one-bedroom apartment, listening to soft music. Neither of them wanted to watch TV. Their first-floor apartment in the university's graduate student housing was inexpensively but tastefully done up—some artwork on the walls, a lamp from a thrift store in the corner, and a colorful Guatemalan cloth covering the dinner table. The thumping started suddenly in the apartment above theirs, as it did some evenings. Tim and Becky, who lived upstairs, were also graduate students at the university, and good friends of the Zimbys. They had all graduated from the same college together and had known each other for years. But both Peter and Mary found it strange that Tim would not go to the university gym to exercise and instead jump up and down in his apartment. And every day the thumping of the floor as he exercised would begin at the same time. Today, however, amid the thumping, they heard Becky's screaming and sobbing. Peter and Mary looked at each other—they suddenly realized that what they had assumed to be the sounds of a man exercising were most likely the sounds of domestic violence. What should they do? Call the police based on suspicion and ruin a good friend's life? Go up and confront Tim, who could potentially be in a bad state of mind and turn violent?

/////////////

TODAY'S WORLD IS best described by one word: "turbulence." Whether we are talking of business climates or our own personal lives, change is all around us. We are buffeted by ever-changing technological winds; globalization is opening unexplored markets at the same time that it is dramatically altering existing ones; political instability and governmental policy are creating tremendous uncertainty; competition cannot be foreseen and often originates from unexpected quarters; and customers are fickle and their preferences unpredictable. Patterns of labor migration and increasing rates of employee attrition only serve to compound this problem. These are only a few of the many unforeseeable forces that impact organizations today. And of course turbulence in the business environment has economic and human implications for our everyday lives.

Life, both for you personally and for your company, is marked by a string of curveballs, inflection points, disruptions, and the like—and, like everything in life, some of these unpredicted happenings are positive and some are negative. Your company could suddenly face an unexpected labor strike or a sudden choking of its supply chain. On the other hand, a new technology may be able to help you create an exciting innovation. A change in government may open up new market opportunities or bring stricter regulations. Similarly, at the personal level, for you, a critical subordinate may resign. Your team may become embroiled in a communication crisis with a key customer. An unanticipated promotion may open up a new leadership opportunity.

CEOs everywhere are seeking ways to capitalize on unforeseen opportunities and to cope with unanticipated hurdles. Unfortunately, in a world where the unforeseen and unanticipated are happening at a faster and faster pace, older ideologies and familiar methods are proving grossly inadequate; organizations and executives need new paradigms and new frameworks. And the need is urgent.

In this context, this book will help you in two ways. First, it will teach you how you and your organization can develop capabilities, not only to survive and succeed, but to emerge as leaders and sustain leadership positions even in conditions that are characterized by unpredictability, risk, and deep uncertainty. Second, rather than just teach you how to be reactive and agile in the short term, this book will teach you how to be successful in the long term with a sustained strategy.

Let me elaborate. As I said before, it has become common business wisdom that in today's turbulent circumstances we need to develop agility—the ability to *quickly adapt* to changing environments and circumstances. But simply having agility isn't enough. Consider the story of this company that demonstrated tremendous supply chain agility.

A Fiery Test of Agility

Around 8:00 p.m. on March 17, 2000, the Dutch company Philips NV faced an "act of God" disaster different from the one that destroyed the EID Parry factory. Philips's semiconductor chip manufacturing facility in Albuquerque caught fire after a lightning strike created electrical surges across the state of New Mexico. The fire was put out in less than ten minutes by the factory's automatically activated sprinklers and by the trained factory staff. The damage seemed minimal at first: eight trays of silicon wafers were destroyed in the clean room—the wafer-producing facility that is kept thousands of times cleaner than operating theaters in hospitals. The thought that these eight trays would have produced radio-frequency chips for thousands of cell phones was sobering. But more significant was the damage inflicted by the water and smoke on the clean room itself. Philips estimated a week's delay in production and proceeded to inform its two major clients—for now, let's call them company A and its competitor, company B. Forty percent of the chips from this factory went to these two clients, and they were the main customers who were going to be affected.

Company B, upon receiving the news about the fire and the shipment delay, quickly examined its inventory positions. It determined that it had enough chips in stock to tide over the week's delay—such delays, it knew, were routine in the tight supply situations that marked the semiconductor-manufacturing industry. And thus it waited for the Philips factory to be restored.

Company A, on the other hand, went into classic fire-fighting mode. It first set up a team to monitor the progress of the repairs to the factory with Philips. A few days later, it realized that the problem was much larger than Philips had initially estimated. When it became clear that supplies from the New Mexico factory would take longer in coming than initially estimated, company A immediately did three things. First, it scoured the chip-manufacturing world for other suppliers and grabbed up chips wherever they were available—including Southeast

Asia. Second, with CEO-level negotiations, it got Philips to rearrange production in its factories in Asia to be able to manufacture chips for company A's phones. And third, it redesigned portions of the critical chip so that it could be manufactured in other plants—both Philips and non-Philips.

By the time company B woke up to the seriousness of the situation and started to look for other manufacturers, it found that company A had cornered all the chips available on the market. The Philips factory took six weeks to get back in action. At the end of that operating quarter, company B reported that it had suffered a $200 million operating loss as a result of the shortage of chips. Six months later, in its annual report, it declared that it had suffered a 3 percent loss in its mobile phone market share, and that its mobile phone division had incurred a loss of $1.68 billion (pulling the overall company to an operating loss of $167 million). Company B never recovered from this, and ultimately, in 2001, it ended up selling its phone division to another company. Company A, on the other hand, went on to become, over the next few years, the biggest cell phone manufacturer in the world, commanding a huge 50 percent market share in 2007.

The Agility Puzzle

The incident of the fire in the Philips factory and its aftermath is often used as an example to show how a company that is agile (company A) reaches the pinnacle of success while a company that lacks agility (company B) fails dismally. An article in the *Wall Street Journal* epitomized this assessment of the two companies. Among other causes, it claimed that company A responded to the fire incident with "a characteristic Finnish curtness under pressure—the Finns call it *sisu*—that signaled they meant business." However, this conclusion comes from a short-term perspective, as the revelation of the names of these companies will indicate. If you have not already recognized them, company A is Nokia, and company B is Ericsson, whose cell phone division was acquired by Sony to form Sony-Ericsson. As this episode demonstrates, Nokia was celebrated for its supply chain agility. As it turns out, the critical word in the previous sentence is not "agility" but "was." Because Nokia, the wireless-handset company, does not exist today.

The understanding that agility is a driver of competitiveness in turbulent environments is itself called into question by Nokia's struggles and dismal performance over the last few years, which culminated in its selling its devices business to Microsoft in late 2013. In fact, Nokia's fall has been extraordinary and fast. Even as recently as 2008, its share of the worldwide market for handheld mobile phones was a dizzying 50 percent. Nokia's share of the smartphone market dramatically declined from more than 50 percent in 2007 to less than 5 percent in 2013. Nokia's return-on-assets performance was also dismal. It declined from nearly 25 percent in 2007 to *negative* 10 percent in 2012. Return on assets is a significant measure because it is a commentary on the company's management practice.[6] So at the end of all this we are left with a puzzle: if Nokia was remarkably agile, as it demonstrated in the aftermath of the fire incident in the Philips factory, why did it fail?

The Concept of Strategic Agility

The answer to why Nokia failed lies in the fact that there is more to agility than meets the eye. With 20/20 hindsight, today we can say that while Nokia demonstrated tremendous supply chain flexibility, it was, in fact, not agile in many other ways. As several business thinkers have argued, Nokia was not sensitive to customer preferences. For instance, it did not produce a clamshell phone despite the incredible success of

> *There is more to agility than meets the eye.*

Motorola's Razr in the US market. It refused to move from the proprietary Symbian operating system, which did not adequately support smartphone applications, and when it did move, it chose to go with a Microsoft operating system despite the popularity and promise of the emerging Android operating system.

Simply put, *agility is never about just one thing*; organizations always operate in business contexts that are inherently multidimensional and complex. We need an appropriately sophisticated understanding of agility—a concept that we call in this book *strategic agility.* Strategic agility makes the concept of agility comprehensive by locating it in the realm of long-term planning in the face of a quickly unfolding unknown—an unknown that is not only about risk but also about uncertainty and, sometimes, about unknowable, deep uncertainty. The term "strategic agility" combines two contradictory concepts: strategic implies slow-moving and long-term, while agility connotes speedy, short-term orientation. In essence, the term forces us to hold concepts that are in seeming opposition as we think about business moves— and dealing with ambiguity is critically necessary in today's business environments.

In this book I present the Vivékin Intelligences Framework, which enables leaders and companies to develop strategic agility. The quintessential driver of human adaptability—*intelligence*—inspires the framework, which developed during years of my research at Wharton, and the business schools at Purdue University and the University of Minnesota. It incorporates findings from many fields of research—from evolutionary economics and ethnography to psychology, operations management, and business strategy.

Using advances made in research in these diverse fields, I will show that companies need to develop multiple kinds of agilities and cultivate an enhanced sensitivity to context so they can apply the combination of agilities that is most appropriate to the situation. The framework you'll discover encompasses both a *people* aspect and an *organizational* aspect. This implies that strategic agility brings together two fields that were traditionally thought to be separate: leadership development and competitive strategy.

The Vivékin Intelligences Framework will help you assess yourself and your organization to determine flexibilities in five different dimensions. It will guide you in leveraging your strong agilities and strengthening your weaker agilities. It will also enable you to design context-appropriate dynamic strategies so you can develop into a flexible leader and also transform your company into an agile and resilient industry leader—and to do it all in the face of rapid change.

Chapter 2

Intelligence-Driven Agility

ABOUT 10,000–11,500 YEARS AGO, the first humans arrived on the North American continent using a land bridge to cross what we today call the Bering Strait—the small strip of sea that separates Russia from Alaska. Paleontologists believe that a corridor opened up between giant ice sheets covering what is now Alaska and Alberta, making possible the journey of these first North Americans. These immigrants, now known collectively as Clovis people, spread quickly through the North American continent, going southward across the Great Plains and the southwestern states, even as far as New Mexico. In fact, since the early 1900s several archaeological finds in New Mexico have uncovered evidence of this migration through items such as spearheads big enough to kill large animals. Not only is the advent of humans into North America remarkable for the extent of its spread across the continent, but also amazing is the *speed* at which this migration happened.

Eleven thousand years is not such a long time in evolutionary history. So the first humans in North America were not very different from you and me. In fact, some BBC documentaries depict these Clovis people as very much like today's nomads. Life, however, was not easy for the Clovis people, especially given their lack of resources as compared, for example, with the large Ice Age animals that populated the North American continent then. The animals they had to kill for food were huge game like giant bison and the woolly mammoth; the size of these animals demanded specialized hunting skills— a significant challenge given that all the Clovis people had for weapons were sticks and stones.

Another fearsome animal, the saber-toothed tiger, also populated the North American continent. It was about the present tiger's size but much more powerfully built. It had strong forearms and a mouth that could open wide enough to grip the necks of the big Ice Age herbivores. The saber-toothed tiger hunted by pinning down its prey and going straight for the jugular with its two nine-inch-long, stiletto-like teeth. Death was perhaps relatively painless, but definite. The genus name for the saber-toothed tiger is *Smilodon*, which comes from the Greek words for "knife tooth."

But if we fast-forward ten thousand years, there are no woolly mammoths or giant bison. There are no saber-toothed tigers. Of course, there *are* humans. How did the Clovis people, with their scarce resources, survive against these odds? And how did they rapidly migrate across the continent from the ice sheets of Alaska through the Great Plains of the Midwest to the mountains of New Mexico? These questions hold important lessons for organizations and individuals competing against rivals with larger and better resources in times of great turbulence (even if the turbulence isn't quite as dramatic as the Ice Age).

The Clovis spearheads discovered in the early part of the twentieth century provide a clue to this puzzle: these palm-sized spearheads had added fluting that made them deadly enough to kill large Ice Age animals. In fact, these specialized spearheads, sharpened on both sides and with unique fluting at the base that made them easy to attach to spear shafts, have come to be known as Clovis points. Evidence found at the various sites where Clovis points have been discovered indicates that Clovis people were highly skilled big-game hunters. Further, paleontologists believe that Clovis people were intelligent, enterprising, and quite advanced culturally. They had unique technology that allowed them to create the Clovis point and various other specialized cutting tools; they appear to have grown plants to meet the increasing demands to feed a growing population; they developed ways to work as teams as they hunted the big game and overcame adversaries such as the saber-toothed tiger. From all this comes the conclusion that the Clovis people survived and thrived in adverse conditions of varying intensity primarily because of their *intelligence*.

So, the remarkable, if unrecognized, lesson for us as we try to develop capabilities to deal with turbulent environments lies in understanding and developing a framework around intelligence. Intelligence allows us to work and succeed in changing circumstances even when we do not have adequate resources.

Take a moment right now to try a test:

Imagine that you're on your way to an important meeting and when you reach the airport, you discover that the flight has been canceled. What do you do? List all the possible solutions you can come up with.

When I ask this question in workshops, participants come up with a range of answers, some of which might be running through your mind right now: seek an alternate flight; find another means of transport; call your counterparts to see if you can reschedule the meeting; explore whether you can use videoconferencing technology to conduct the meeting; and so on. Each of these solutions is based on having a piece of knowledge that exists in your head: you know there are alternate flights, you know there are other means of transport, you know that you have some leeway in scheduling the meeting, or you know that videoconferencing technology can enable a remote meeting. When you make a choice among these options, you are essentially choosing to work with the most appropriate piece of knowledge given the context.

So far, management thinking has led us to understand that the primary driver of competitive advantage, especially in the information age, is knowledge. That's why you hear about the knowledge-based organization, the knowledge worker, and the various knowledge-prefixed terms that abound in business jargon. Yes, indeed, knowledge is a tremendous resource. But what we are beginning to realize is that in fast-paced dynamic environments, knowledge creates two problems. First, it can become dated, and thus trap us in old ways of thinking and doing. Imagine if astrophysicists today used scientific knowledge that was current in the fourteenth century, and believed that all bodies in space revolve around the earth! Second, knowledge can be inadequate or simply not there. For example, your company may have never worked with mobile commerce; it does not know the underlying technology, and it does not know what potential this technology has for service delivery. How can you create a mobile-commerce strategy in the absence of knowledge? You may face similar situations in your own life. Suppose you are an executive posted to a new country—you do not know the language or the culture. How do you emerge as a leader?

We need to conceptualize the dynamic, flexible, learning organization of tomorrow around a new paradigm: *the intelligence-driven organization.* Similarly, we need to think of the leader of tomorrow not only as a person with knowledge, but also as *the intelligence-driven leader.*

The New Paradigm: The Intelligence-Driven Organization

An intelligence-oriented perspective allows us to conceptualize an adaptable and agile organization in new ways. First, it frees the company from being rooted in a certain technology or practice. The knowledge that gave the company its strategic advantage and competitive value can itself become a trap in turbulent environments. For example, in the 1980s minicomputer firms such as DEC and Wang Labs dominated the technology landscape, but they couldn't move out of that mind-set when PCs came in the 1990s, and as a result they do not exist today.

An intelligence-driven organization, on the other hand, is constantly learning, constantly adapting. It dynamically and appropriately uses and recombines resources, acquires new ones, or even sometimes divests resources to continuously generate competitive advantage in changing business contexts.

Second, an intelligence-oriented perspective brings the human to the center of our idea of the firm and allows us to consider leadership, innovation, and strategy in one framework. This is a very important move, because it is becoming apparent that in a dynamic, fast-moving environment we cannot think of strategy, leadership, and value innovation as separate from one another. Nimble companies need nimble people.

> *Nimble companies need nimble people.*

The Nimble Organization of the Future: The Intelligence-Driven Company

Consider a company that for six consecutive years, from 1996 to 2001, was named America's Most Innovative Company by *Fortune* magazine. Its founder-president had a PhD in economics and was considered an outstanding expert in his industry. Its chief executive officer was a brilliant Baker Scholar from the Harvard Business School, graduating in the top 5 percent of his class. The chief financial officer was another brilliant MBA, from the famous Kellogg School of Management at Northwestern University. Apart from seeing it as wickedly innovative, the general public perceived this company as one of the best managed—in fact, as one of the greatest companies in the world. The company even established a prize for distinguished public service, and among the recipients of this award were Nelson Mandela, Mikhail Gorbachev, Colin Powell, and Alan Greenspan. And yet within a few months, in late 2001, as its murky story unfolded, this company, Enron, folded. The sophisticated chicanery and ingenuity it had applied to its accounting practices were exposed—it had used its agility to fool the public and the stock market for many years.

Enron can be described as a very agile company: it responded quickly to changing market situations, it exploited new market opportunities, and it handled crises in innovative ways. It did not lack for smart people who had tremendous knowledge. However, companies like Enron and Nokia were not able to sustain their competitive advantage in the medium term, let alone the long term. If you recall, I said earlier that *intelligence drives agility*. Taking lessons from Nokia and Enron, we see that these companies focused on particular kinds of agility: Nokia on supply chain agility (operational), and Enron on financial agility (analytical). Such a narrow focus won't work because we don't know what kind of challenge the turbulent world is going to throw at us. We may be great at supply chain agility, but the demand may be for rapid adjustments in marketing.

Once we recognize the connection between intelligence and agility, we see that recent advances in theories of intelligence offer great insights into a framework of agilities. I will discuss briefly in the next section the theory of multiple intelligences, which argues that there are many kinds of intelligence. Each of us may be good at some and not so good at others. Drawing on this, we realize that in order to be competitive in the long run, individuals and organizations need to develop different kinds of agilities. I have found that we need five agilities: analytical, operational, inventive, communicative, and visionary. While analytical, operational, inventive, and communicative agilities drive short-term responses, visionary agility helps the organization to consider problems and solutions in the longer term and to adopt a wider perspective. Just as you can mix the three primary colors to get any color, agile leaders, whether they are companies or individuals, mix four agilities—analytical, operational, inventive, and communicative—in the proportion that best suits the context. Visionary agility is the medium with which the colors are mixed—you cannot paint an agile picture without the visionary component, as Nokia and Enron discovered the hard way.

A Very Brief History of Intelligence Research

Beginning in the 1980s, educational psychology saw a dramatic shift in the conceptualization of intelligence. From the 1920s, intelligence had become entwined with the notion of IQ—a measure that tested an individual's analytic and logical skills—and in fact IQ testing had become a massive industry. From the 1990s, Howard Gardner at Harvard and Robert Sternberg at Yale argued for an understanding of intelligence that went beyond the narrow constraints of IQ. Gardner's multiple-intelligences theory views intelligence as comprising eight different intelligences while Sternberg's triarchic theory argues that we have three different kinds of intelligences: analytical, creative, and practical (street smarts). Applying these theories of intelligence to organizational contexts and reworking them, I found that great companies and great leaders develop and use five intelligences, which drive five agilities.

Bear, Dinosaur, Cheetah, Human

Management literature and business thinking have typically conceptualized agility as a unitary construct: companies are successful because their agility enables them to handle turmoil or turbulence. "Agility" has become a catchall term: it encompasses supply chain or manufacturing flexibilities, innovation capabilities, and even the capacity to handle mergers and acquisitions. As we consider practical ways to make companies agile, such broad-stroke definitions of agility do not help. As we saw in chapter 1, the story of Nokia is illustrative. The New Mexico fire incident led observers to believe that Nokia was a tremendously agile company; however, its lack of multiple agilities, and perhaps an overreliance on one kind of agility, led ultimately to its downfall.

Despite Nokia's example, management literature for the most part has not engaged with the concept of multiple agilities in an organization. The Vivékin Agility Matrix[7] allows us to position people and companies along dimensions of both agility and context sensitivity. As shown in the table, you can position your company (or yourself) in the following matrix. Your company may be agile or not agile; if it's agile, it may have a single agility or multiple agilities. Whether or not it's agile, it can be context sensitive.

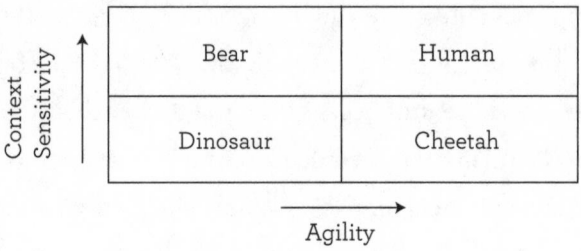

The Vivékin Agility Matrix

"Dinosaurs" are companies that are rich in resources but neither agile nor context sensitive. They continue to operate even when their resources and capabilities are irrelevant. Such companies soon find themselves on the way to extinction. Companies in the minicomputer industry like DEC, Data General, and Wang Labs are classic examples of dinosaurs: they were rich in resources and tremendously successful but did not change with the technology and market trends, and went bankrupt one after another. "Bears" are companies that are rich in resources and capabilities but, like the dinosaurs, they are not agile. However, in contrast to the dinosaurs, they are context sensitive— they become aware that they cannot compete in the changed business climate. So they go into hibernation during the business winter and reemerge when conditions suit their resources. "Cheetahs" are very agile but are context insensitive—they are companies that rely dangerously on a single agility. A cheetah—natural running machine that it is—can only hunt by running down its prey on the vast open savannas. It is very inflexible in other ways: it cannot hunt in the dark or climb trees, for instance. As I discussed earlier, Nokia is a classic example of this kind of single agility, which, in an ironic way, can become a hindrance to the competitiveness of the firm. The ideal companies, those with strategic agility, are the "humans"—they have multiple agilities and are also context sensitive. A strategically agile company recombines resources dynamically, invents new resources when it needs them, pools resources with others when necessary—in short, it demonstrates multiple agilities that it uses according to context.

As mentioned, the five agilities in the Vivékin Intelligences Framework are analytical, operational, inventive, communicative, and visionary.

> **Analytical agility** allows a company to change the means and methods of analysis. For instance, a company can adapt to and exploit new tax regulations to gain a competitive advantage because it has analytical agility, or it can shift between multiple budget justification processes depending on the kind of project being considered.

Operational agility helps the company gain dynamism through its operational resources. Examples of this are seen in flexible production systems, supply chain flexibility, and dynamic collaborative arrangements.

Inventive agility enables the generation of new ideas, creative solutions, and alternate uses of resources to solve problems the company has not seen before or to take advantage of new opportunities the company faces.

Communicative agility is the skill a company has to persuade its audiences and to convey the value of its ideas through words and speech. Advertising campaigns and taglines offer immediate illustrations of this agility.

Visionary agility allows the company to recognize the long-term impact of the decisions it is making. It also checks for the breadth of impact, asking questions such as, how many people or issues are being affected, and in what ways? It thus makes the company adopt a "beyond-me, beyond-profit-line" perspective that gives agility its strategic quality. Those companies that use visionary agility to vet the agile solutions proposed by the other agilities achieve success both in the short term and in the long term.

Companies and Individuals as Nimble Pioneers

The concept of intelligence as a driver of agility immediately offers a possible solution to a long-standing question in strategic management: where and how do we build dynamic capabilities in organizations? As is obvious from the discussion so far, intelligence brings into discussions of strategy a human dimension, implying that the intelligences must be developed not only in organizational processes, structures, and technologies but also in people. Not surprisingly, there are interesting human stories that parallel the stories about organizations I have presented before. Consider, for example, the story of Winston Churchill, which is very much like the story of Nokia.

Winston Churchill: Rigid Leader

When World War II ended in Europe in May 1945, opinion polls showed Winston Churchill's approval ratings to be a remarkable 83 percent. Few prime ministers could boast of such great ratings. And, of course, Churchill's popularity was not without reason. He had pulled the British back from the jaws of defeat and on to a painful but glorious victory. The long overdue British elections were scheduled for June 1945, and, with such popularity ratings, Churchill was expected to win handily. However, the British public, shockingly enough, voted him and his Conservative Party out of office pretty convincingly. Why did Churchill lose? How did Clement Attlee of the Labour Party become a giant killer? Some political analysts and leadership theorists have argued that Churchill lost "because the very qualities that had made him a great leader in war were ill-suited to domestic politics in peacetime."[8]

The famous leadership-studies scholar Warren Bennis, at the University of Southern California, provides an answer. In the second edition of his classic book *On Becoming a Leader*, Bennis writes, "The one competence that I now realize is absolutely essential for leaders—the key competence—is adaptive capacity. Adaptive capacity is what allows leaders to respond quickly and intelligently to relentless change."[9] This is very similar to the BP CEO John Browne's exhortation: "All you can do is to give yourself the capacity to respond to the only certainty in life—which is uncertainty. The creation of that capability is the purpose of strategy."[10] In turbulent times, what is demanded of the organization parallels what is demanded of people.

Strategically agile leaders—whether they are individuals or organizations—are persuasive when they need to be and also readily jump into action when necessary; they can be policy wonks when the context calls for it, or they can be creative geniuses; but above all they are visionary, thinking of the larger good of their followers and of the world. Two case studies below—one about an individual and the other about a company—will illustrate how such leaders develop and apply all five agilities, combining them in ways that are most appropriate to the situation. I won't call out which agility is at work at every point in the two stories—that would become very didactic—but will for the most part allow you to discern which agilities are being employed as the stories progress.

Roy Vagelos Takes on River Blindness in Africa

Dr. Roy Vagelos joined Merck & Co., one of the world's leading pharmaceutical companies, in 1975 as the senior vice president of research. Before joining Merck, Dr. Vagelos had been the chair of the Department of Biological Chemistry at the School of Medicine at Washington University. In 1978 a research scientist in his lab, William Campbell, came to him with what seemed to be a remarkable discovery—a possible cure for the disease river blindness. A drug was working for livestock, and Campbell wanted permission to develop the drug for human use. River blindness was plaguing large populations in West Africa, turning entire communities blind and cutting life expectancies in the villages along the banks of rivers. Tiny flies transmit the disease by injecting parasitic larvae into humans through bites. These larvae spread prodigiously through the skin and cause severe irritation, and soon go into the eyes, setting off a blindness that progresses irrevocably. Children in these communities would be born with sight but begin to lose it by the time they were young adults. Total blindness would set in by middle age. There were also many cases of children completely losing their vision. About 20 million people struggled with river blindness, and increasing numbers became exposed to it every day. Scientists across the world were struggling to find a cure. William Campbell's discovery was therefore momentous.

But for Roy Vagelos, the director of research, and his approval committee, the project was fraught with risk. Antiparasitic drugs did not usually succeed across species—just because Merck was making and selling the drug successfully for use in horses did not guarantee success in humans. Moreover, if the side effects in human application proved to be severe, the sales of the animal product would also be drastically affected. Scientists involved in the animal drug development and sales warned Vagelos that approving human trials for the drug would be very unwise. On the other hand, Vagelos knew that Merck's scientists, who believed they were on the verge of a scientific breakthrough, would be demoralized if the human trials were not approved. More than that, nonapproval would go against the company's principles, which prioritized health over wealth. Vagelos gave the go-ahead for human trials.

By 1987 the human trials were showing remarkable medical benefits with minimal side effects, and Roy Vagelos therefore applied for commercial approval. By now he was the CEO of Merck, having been promoted to that position in 1985. It was not an easy decision, however, to produce the miracle drug to cure river blindness. It was very clear that the poor African communities would not be able to pay for the drug, and thus Merck would never be able to sell the drug, which cost more than three dollars per tablet. The cost for the first year to move the drug from the lab through production into the distribution chain would itself be two million dollars, and then year after year, the annual cost to supply the drug would exceed twenty million.

Vagelos set out to seek external funding. The United States Agency for International Development (USAID) heard Vagelos's argument that it would be an inexpensive way to establish American presence in Africa but responded with a refrain that Vagelos would hear from every possible funding source: "We don't have any money." Vagelos sought money from various governments across the world, but without success. The World Health Organization (WHO) had a response similar to USAID's but went further—WHO's Brian Duke made a public statement that Merck should give away the drug for free.

Although he was disappointed with the WHO statement—what commercial organization would think of giving products away free?—Vagelos felt it was a moral duty to do just that. But he still had to convince the board of directors. To do this, Vagelos went back in Merck's history, to a period immediately after World War II. In the years after the war, Japan was reeling with outbreaks of tuberculosis, and although Merck already had a very powerful drug to treat it, streptomycin, very few people could pay for it. Merck had then decided to donate a large supply of the drug to Japan. This generous act was not forgotten, and when, decades later, Merck wanted to acquire a majority stake in Japan's drugmaker Banyu Pharmaceutical, despite the horrendously closed market, Japan approved the deal. Using this as an example, Vagelos convinced the Merck board of directors in 1988 that giving the river blindness drug away for free was the best thing to do in the current scenario and keeping in mind the future. The *New York Times* announced on October 22, 1987: "Merck & Company announced today that it had developed a drug to cure river blindness and would distribute it free of cost to countries that request it." Thus Merck gave away the river blindness drug for free, and Merck and Roy Vagelos became heroes across Africa. Perhaps most important, this decision was in complete harmony with the company's principles.

EID Parry Clears Up After Cyclone Thane

Let's go back to the story of the Indian sugar company EID Parry, which I began in chapter 1. To review, in late December 2011, Cyclone Thane hit the region and EID's biggest factory at Nellikuppam lay directly in its path. When the storm was over, the factory's roof had been blown off, and four thousand acres of sugarcane lay flattened. EID Parry had to process ten thousand tons of sugarcane in ten days because the shelf life of sugarcane is limited. Initial estimates suggested that it would take at least thirty days for the plant to become operational. EID Parry got the plant running and finished crushing the cane in five days flat. The story of how it did this offers a vivid illustration of organizational agilities at work.

Let's get a little bit of background first. EID Parry is a South Indian sugar company with annual revenues of 15.37 billion rupees. It is part of the Murugappa Group of companies and has its corporate headquarters in Chennai. Every day its five factories in Tamil Nadu and Puducherry crush more than nineteen thousand tons of sugarcane and, as by-products, generate eighty-two megawatts of power and distill up to 135 kiloliters of alcohol. The company sources its sugarcane from about one hundred thousand farmers, who grow sugarcane on farms that cover about two hundred thousand acres.

When Cyclone Thane hit the EID Parry factory in December 2011, the managing director, Ravindra Singhvi, was away on a short vacation. He rushed back the same day and visited the site; he could not believe the destruction. Apart from the factory, the housing complex was also badly damaged, and EID staff families were left without electricity and water. Singhvi and his executives decided that the first priority should be the families, because no employee was going to be able to concentrate on work with his or her family suffering at home. They mobilized staff and resources from other plants, and work began immediately. Diesel-run generators were brought from other factories; some were even purchased or rented. By the end of the first day, they had restored power to the residences. Then Singhvi met the chairman of the Tamil Nadu Electricity Board (TNEB) who promised to send a senior executive to supervise the restoration of power to the sugarcane farms. But Singhvi made an unusual request: Could the senior executive work under the guidance of EID executives, because they knew best where power was most needed and where it was less needed? The TNEB chairman agreed to this request, and as a result power was restored to farmers in a very efficient way.

Since food and water were major issues, EID arranged for food to be cooked in Chennai, and it established a transport system to take the food and fresh water to the factory areas for a few days. Vans ferried cooked food every day—sometimes two times a day—covering the twenty-eight-mile stretch from the kitchens in Chennai to the factory in Nellikuppam in less than two hours. Everybody worked round the clock, and the factory was up and running in a couple of days. The crushing was completed in five days. Then EID Parry did something unusual that is a classic illustration of visionary agility.

Generally, sugarcane loses juice content rapidly after it is harvested. But in this case, the problem was compounded: the cane was not fully grown and already had been stored for a few days, so the juice yield had come down significantly. However, EID Parry paid its farmers the same price it would have for good sugarcane. In the process, it suffered a loss of 45 million rupees (roughly 1 million US dollars at the time). Why is this visionary agility?

For EID Parry, its farmers are not suppliers but partners. The company advises the farmers throughout cultivation about what to plant, how to use technologies like drip irrigation, how to fertilize, and what pesticides to use. It has recently established a three-hundred-person call center farmers can contact with questions. As a result, growing the cane becomes much easier for the farmer. In an exhibition of analytical agility, the company has created a rare financial arrangement in which it acts as a guarantor to banks for loans farmers take for equipment and agricultural services. These loans currently total 8.5 billion rupees. Demonstrating a combination of agilities, EID has also helped some of its farmers become entrepreneurs by helping them buy expensive equipment, which they then rent out to other farmers. To overcome labor shortages, the company has arranged a pool of twenty-five thousand laborers who can be hired by farmers in groups of twenty.

The conscious development and deployment of these

agilities has become strategy for EID Parry with long-term benefits. Its farms have a 20 percent higher yield: thirty-two tons per acre compared with the national average of twenty-seven tons per acre. Moreover, its relationship with its farmers ensures that the latter do not abandon it for other factories or for other crops. In fact, EID has changed the running period of a sugar factory from the traditional 180 days to 300 days, taking advantage of the Tamil Nadu climate. EID is guaranteed procurement of the additional cane required because of its relationship with its farmers. In fact, while many sugar factories are dreading the potential liberalization of the sugar industry, in which farmers will become free to associate with any sugar factory of their choice, EID is looking forward to it—its use of the five agilities has guaranteed that its farmers will not stray; in fact, other farmers want to bring their sugarcane to EID. Visionary agility at work—in the short term and way beyond.

Chapter 3

//

Analytical Agility: Understanding the Real Problem

W E CAN SOMETIMES POINT to a particular date on which humankind made a pathbreaking advancement. July 20, 1969, was one such day. As Neil Armstrong took his first steps across the face of the moon, his words, "That's one small step for man, one giant leap for mankind," became etched in history. Armstrong and his Apollo 11 colleague Buzz Aldrin landed in the Sea of Tranquility on the moon in a small landing module; Michael Collins orbited the moon in the command spacecraft until Armstrong and Aldrin rejoined him the next day for their joint return to earth. A few months later, Pete Conrad and Alan Bean of the Apollo 12 team repeated this feat—they landed on the moon again, and this time they walked across the Ocean of Storms.

On April 11, 1970—barely nine months after Apollo 11—the Apollo 13 mission executed a picture-perfect takeoff. The spacecraft *Odyssey* had begun its expedition to the moon very well indeed. Its mission was more ambitious than previous missions—the goal of Apollo 11 and Apollo 12 had been to show that it was possible to put men on the moon and bring them safely back to earth. The spaceship *Odyssey*, with its three astronauts—Jim Lovell (the commander), Fred Haise, and Jack Swigert—was targeted to land in the Fra Mauro Highlands, a hilly region near the Mare Imbrium—the second largest crater on the moon. After landing, Apollo 13 would bring back lunar rocks and other material that would help scientists unravel many mysteries—both about the moon's formation and its elemental composition.

Nearly fifty-six hours into the mission, everything was going according to plan. Apollo 13 was two hundred thousand miles from Earth and forty-five thousand miles from the moon; it was entering the "lunar sphere of influence," where the moon's gravity becomes stronger than Earth's. So smoothly had the flight progressed till then that the Mission Control engineer Joe Kerwin complained to Lovell over the radio, "We're bored to tears down here." Thus when Fred Haise began, "Okay, Houston," and Jack Swigert completed the somewhat alarmed announcement, "I believe we've had a problem here," Jack Lousma, the engineer at Mission Control who was communicating with Swigert, was nonplussed. "This is Houston. Say again, please," he requested. Now Jim Lovell's voice came through with bone-chilling clarity: "Houston, we've had a problem. We've had a main B bus undervolt." *Odyssey* was suffering a major loss of its electrical power.

It quickly came to light that one of the two oxygen tanks on *Odyssey* had exploded, cutting off oxygen supply to two of the three banks of fuel cells—as a result, one of the two main voltage buses, the main bus B, was not carrying electricity. The loss of an oxygen tank was not something to be dismissed—it would mean that *Odyssey* would be short of both oxygen and electrical power. The other oxygen tank, which was powering main bus A, would still see them through, Lovell thought, as he peered through the window. He radioed what he saw: "We're venting something out into the . . . into space," and trailed off as he realized that the only remaining oxygen tank was also leaking. As a sense of the catastrophe descended upon Lovell, the engineers at Mission Control in Houston were equally alarmed by what they saw on their instruments and monitors—they estimated that the astronauts had very little time till the command module lost all its power. The first thing they did was to get the three astronauts to move from the command module into the lunar module, the small craft that was to land on the moon; it was designed to hold two people for two days on the moon while the service module and the command module orbited the moon. Now it had to hold three people for up to four days. And thus began what has been simultaneously called NASA's most significant challenge and its finest hour—a three-day heroic mission to bring back to Earth three astronauts trapped in a failing spaceship that was three-quarters of the way to the moon.

That the NASA team succeeded in that mission, and did so spectacularly, is a triumph of human nature. As Alan Shepard and Donald "Deke" Slayton note, "If Lovell and his crew were to survive, Mission Control had just hours to perform calculations and make engineering recommendations that would normally have required weeks."[11] Mission Control managed this incredible task, and Lovell, Haise, and Swigert were brought back to Earth safely. Others have recounted the story very well, both in print (Jim Lovell's own recounting, *Lost Moon*, and Michael Useem's *Leadership Moment*, for example) and on film (Ron Howard's 1995 movie *Apollo 13* featuring Tom Hanks as Jim Lovell).

NASA's actions can be seen as a breathtaking unfolding of combinations of the five agilities over the three dramatic days of the rescue. In each of the accounts mentioned above, one person, flight director Eugene Kranz, emerges as the epitome of leadership under fire.

According to NASA policy, the ultimate responsibility for the flight was with the flight director, and so the task of getting the astronauts safely back home rested on Gene Kranz's shoulders. Wearing his trademark white vest, Kranz was the quintessential leader; his tension was palpable, but at the same time he remained supremely calm while making decisions—assimilating information from different sources, making decisions in very little time, and issuing orders to different engineers in the various units of NASA's Mission Control group. He is credited with getting the team of bright NASA engineers to work together and achieve what had seemed humanly impossible. The entire three-day event shows how Gene Kranz used the five agilities in ways that fit the different situations in which he found himself. I want to focus on one episode to demonstrate Kranz's outstanding use of analytical agility.

About one day into the crisis, three individuals approached Kranz. Each was superior to him in the organization. The first was Christopher Kraft, his mentor, who was then the deputy director of the entire Manned

Spacecraft Center in Houston. The second was Deke Slayton, a former astronaut who had become director of flight crew operations, and the third—who joined the conversation a little later—was Max Faget, a brilliant inventor, and engineering director of the Manned Spacecraft Center. Each of them had a specific demand that required the astronauts to do something different, and each wanted Kranz to issue orders to have it done immediately. Deke Slayton was concerned that the crew had not slept for a long time and believed very strongly that because of lack of sleep the astronauts would botch up anything they did, especially the critical operations required of them. Chris Kraft, on the other hand, was concerned about conserving power, especially because they were in a battle in which the only resources available to them were those in the tiny lunar module. Kraft combated the argument that the power-down sequence was extraordinarily long and complicated, especially for a sleep-deprived team, with his own: "A sleep period's six hours! Take the crew off stream for that long before powering down, and you're wasting six hours of juice you don't need to waste."[12]

Max Faget had yet another demand for the crew—he wanted them to immediately perform a passive thermal control (PTC) roll before doing anything else. A PTC roll is a maneuver that turns the spaceship over. It had

had one side toward the sun for a long time, while the other side had been facing space. As a result, the side facing the sun was superhot while the side facing space was extremely cold. As Faget put it, without performing the PTC, "we're going to freeze half our systems and cook the other half." Immediately, Kraft and Slayton protested. Kraft argued that the PTC maneuver would put tremendous pressure on whatever little power remained in the spaceship; Slayton added that it would also put tremendous pressure on the astronauts if they were asked to do a PTC roll without sleep.

The three senior NASA officials began to argue with each other in front of Gene Kranz, each trying to convince Kranz to go with his particular game plan. Each had a valid argument for what to do next, and also logical reasons for *not* doing what the other two officials were recommending. The vociferous and well-meaning arguments went on for a few minutes. Kranz had to make a quick decision—should the astronauts sleep, should they power down the spaceship, or should they execute the rollover maneuver? Each action had implications for the others. Time was critical. An immediate decision was needed.

Kranz held up his hand. He announced his decision: the astronauts would do a rollover first, then they would power down the spaceship, and only after that would they get to sleep. He explained, "A tired crew can get over their fatigue, but if we damage this ship any further, we're not going to get over that."

Through the numerous interviews, articles, and books that have appeared on the Apollo 13 crisis, it becomes apparent that Gene Kranz struggled with many critical decisions like the sequencing of sleep, power down, and PTC maneuver. Right at the beginning, Kranz had to make a very tough choice: whether to abort the mission and turn around using whatever power was left in the main spaceship or to go toward and around the moon and use its gravity to propel the lunar module back to Earth. Both decisions were fraught with risk, and it did not help that Kranz's team was split down the middle. Kranz deliberated and chose to go around the moon, because, he reasoned, it gave him more time to make decisions and take actions.[13]

Recognizing the importance of Gene Kranz's leadership in not only rescuing three astronauts but also boosting the morale of NASA and the reputation of America, in 1970 NASA awarded him its Distinguished Service Medal and the US president awarded him and his team the country's highest civilian honor, the Presidential Medal of Freedom. In 1973, NASA bestowed on Kranz its prestigious Outstanding Leadership Medal.

Analytical Intelligence and Analytical Agility

Analytical agility denotes the ability of individuals and organizations to change their analytical patterns and processes as new information becomes available or a new context emerges. It is more than analytical capability—it indicates flexibility in analytical thinking. Can a person or organization *shift between* different kinds of analytical tools or different analytical approaches? An example from the business world will make this distinction clear. In 1980, AT&T commissioned McKinsey & Company to evaluate whether it would be worthwhile to retain its wireless phone lines. As the *Economist* reports: "The consultancy noted all the problems with the new devices— the handsets were absurdly heavy, the batteries kept running out, the coverage was patchy and the cost per minute was exorbitant—and concluded that the total market [in 1999] would be about 900,000."[14] This dismal figure forced AT&T to divest its cellular resources and exit the market.

Unfortunately for AT&T, the cell phone market subsequently exhibited explosive growth, and in 1994 it had to scramble to acquire McCaw Cellular for $12.6 billion in order to reenter the cellular market.[15] In fact, in 1999 there were 109 million users of cell phones—McKinsey's estimate was off by 10,000 percent. Further, the sales data showed that in 1999, 900,000 subscribers were being added *every three days*, and by 2007, 900,000 subscribers were being added every eighteen hours. McKinsey misestimated the number of prospective subscribers, but that does not mean that McKinsey lacked analytical abilities. In fact, it was quite good at analysis. Its estimate was better than Motorola's, which predicted even more conservatively in 1980 that only 270,399 phones would be sold in 2002.[16] And Motorola should have known better because it was the world leader in cell phone technology at the time (1980).

The problem with these analyses is that they used projections based on what they were seeing in the market. The projections would perhaps have been accurate if cell phones were a traditional product, like detergent. McKinsey and the others did not account for the fact that cell phone markets demonstrate network effects, which means that growth will not be linear but exponential—parabolic.

Indeed, the telephone is a classic example of a system that demonstrates network effects. A telephone system that has a single user has virtually no value for that user. However, the addition of an extra user adds tremendous value to both those users, as they can now talk to each other, and with each subsequent user joining the network the value to each existing user increases manifold. At some point, it becomes essential for users outside the system to join in—it becomes impossible to not have a telephone.

Analysts predicting cell phone sales only had to look back in history at the increase in AT&T Bell's subscribers between 1900 and 1910 to understand how such systems work. The parabolic shape of the growth curve of landline telephones between 1905 and 1910 is exactly like the one that describes the growth of cell phones in the late twentieth century.

Thus what McKinsey, Motorola, and others demonstrated was not a lack of analytical ability but a lack of analytical intelligence and, hence, analytical agility. The rigidity of their analytical thinking forced them to resort to regular business projections rather than look at analytical methods that work with exponential growth, such as epidemiology studies where mathematical models had been developed to study the spread of disease among a population, for example. The patterns of growth and mathematical models to predict the growth of the cell phone industry were available in 1980—McKinsey and others did not demonstrate the analytical agility to move from the linear projection models they had successfully used to predict growth in old, established markets to a different model for the emerging and network-effect-dominated cellular market.

What Analytical Agility Does

Analytical agility drives the awareness that is critical to your problem-solving capabilities. It makes you become aware of all the possible options available to solve a problem. Analytical agility helps you understand the "real" problem. It provides an objective analysis of the situation through clear logic and reasoning, leaving little room for emotions that may cloud the situation.

Analytical agility helps you understand the "real" problem.

An example of the clearheaded thinking analytical agility enables is seen in IBM's use of big data—the extremely large data sets that are now available because of the proliferation of websites and interactive devices like cell phones and tablets. The power of big data is that it can be analyzed computationally to reveal hitherto unseen patterns, trends, and associations. In a joint effort, IBM and the Memphis Police Department applied big-data techniques to the data available from rapes in the city, and the analysis led to the discovery of a critical fact: most nighttime rapes occurred when the victim was using a pay phone outside a convenience store or a gas station. This discovery led to a policy change—all pay phones in the city were moved *inside* convenience stores and gas stations. This resulted in a 30 percent drop in incidents of rape.

If you recognize a problem as something that you've solved before, that's analytical agility at work. Analytical agility retrieves solutions tried in the past for similar problems and recalls whether the attempt worked or not. Analytical agility is crucial in helping us to avoid reinventing the wheel. In this sense, analytical agility is the root of learning: it monitors performance in the present and stores in memory whether solutions worked or not. The next time a similar problem arises, your analytical agility will tell you which solution will work and which won't. In engaging in a continuous cycle of problem recognition, solution selection, solution application, and solution monitoring, analytical agility continually creates, uses, and modifies a history of problem solving.

In effect, analytical agility transforms your experience into knowledge. In an organizational context, sometimes this knowledge is made explicit and codified into knowledge bases that are used across the company, but at other times the knowledge remains tacit, confined to you.

Analytical Agility in Action

Analytical agility is very useful whenever a situation or context calls for the application of logical, rational thinking. Often, whether in business or in personal life, problems are not clearly defined; analytical agility helps to pinpoint the real problem in these situations. Any context that requires objective and unbiased judgments, and calls for an ability to shift frames of analysis and examine the problem from different perspectives, is one in which analytical intelligence assumes critical importance.

Anadarko Petroleum

On March 31, 1994, the US Minerals Management Service opened bids for its lease sale of oil and gas fields in the Gulf of Mexico. Called Gulf of Mexico Sale 147, the lease sale had attracted considerable interest because it offered companies the opportunity to purchase drilling rights in a relatively new exploration prospect—subsalt fields in the Gulf of Mexico.

For some years, it was a general conclusion among geologists that vast hydrocarbon deposits were trapped underneath the expansive sheets of salt on the US continental shelf. But recent advances in seismic sensing technology were making the possibility of finding specific reserves of gas and oil beneath the salt layers more real. What was causing even more excitement was the fact that Phillips Petroleum with its two partners—the petroleum giant Amoco and a relatively unknown company called Anadarko Petroleum—had recently made a significant subsalt discovery in another offshore location in the Gulf of Mexico. The Minerals Management Service therefore had anticipated robust and competitive bidding for subsalt exploration rights from various oil and gas companies. But even so, they were not prepared for the explosion of bids—in the previous year (1993), in the same area, sales had totaled $69 million; this year, the sale was touching $277 million. Three companies led the aggressive bidding. Phillips and Amoco, the giant oil exploring companies, were two. The third was Anadarko, a small company. Anadarko was surprisingly aggressive. As an analyst noted: "On a corporate basis, two groups—Amoco on its own or with partners, Anadarko on its own or with partners—each made a sufficient number of bids to indicate that both groups followed a very similar bidding pattern ... but ... the Amoco group was systematically conservative relative to the Anadarko group."[17] Anadarko—either alone or with Phillips—was the top bidder in ten out of the twelve highest sales in the auction.

Of particular interest was the $40 million bid Anadarko made without partners for Ship Shoal South Addition Block 337. That bid was so egregiously high that for one analyst it meant that "either a shift in corporate strategy took place, individual preference overrode exploration assessment procedures, or ... the quality of Anadarko's interpretation for that block was uniquely different [from] that of its partners (Amoco and Phillips) for the same block."

Anadarko won the lease and soon announced a major oil and gas discovery in that field. Today, Anadarko is one of the world's largest independent producers of oil and gas (independent producers are companies that explore for oil and gas around the world but do not refine it).

Michael Cochran, then vice president for worldwide exploration at Anadarko, explained, "Most people looked at it and just saw the minimum case." So what did Anadarko see that others did not? What Anadarko faced in this investment decision was the same thing that confronted every other company—huge potential of an oil or gas discovery characterized by tremendous uncertainty. While other companies approached this decision through the lens of traditional methodologies, such as discounted cash flow (DCF), which computes the net present value (NPV), Anadarko used the new analytical method of "real options," a tool that mimics methods used in pricing options in financial markets.

A real-options method becomes extremely effective in circumstances that are marked by change and uncertainty, situations where the risk predictions that are the basis of the DCF method cannot be made. As Peter Coy wrote in *Business Week* in 1999, "Real-options analysis rewards flexibility—and that's what makes it better than today's standard decision-making tool, 'net present value.' . . . 'Agility.' The New Economy, which is marked by rapid change and lots of uncertainty, cries out for a tool like real options."[18]

A Culture of Analytical Agility

Anadarko has developed a culture that thrives on being analytically agile, on being able to shift between different means and methods of analysis depending on the nature of the situation. As Richard Rowe, then engineering manager at Anadarko, said at a conference in 2000, the goal of Anadarko analysts is to have an array of analytical tools—from DCF and NPV through Monte Carlo simulation to real-option methods—and to use the one that seems most appropriate. When risks are quantifiable in an oil-field bid, use traditional DCF.

When there is tremendous uncertainty, use real-option methods.

John Campbell, president of International Risk Management, remarked in the same discussion, "It is the willingness of people to adopt a new thought process that's the problem. It's senior management, in part, but even at the business unit asset level, there's so much variation in what people are willing to talk about and consider." The culture at Anadarko encouraged this agility.

Shadow Traits of Analytical Agility

I will end this chapter (and each of the next four chapters) with a section that describes what happens when individuals and organizations rely disproportionately on the particular agility in question. While each of the five intelligences and agilities is useful, relying exclusively on one intelligence limits our leadership and organizational agility. Just as everything appears to be a nail to the man who has only a hammer, we tend to use the agility in which we are strongest, regardless of context. We lack the context sensitivity that is essential for us to recognize and apply the appropriate agility or combination of agilities required to solve the problem at hand. And since problems come in all flavors, it is important that our repertoire includes all five intelligences and all five agilities—and that we recognize which one to use when.

There are three primary negative effects if you or your organization focuses too much on solving problems through analytical agility.

Black-and-White Thinking

Ambiguity can become something to fear because the analytically agile mind cannot find a solution to problems that are fuzzy or ambiguous. Some leaders and organizations become fixated on black-and-white thinking: problems must have clear solutions; there is only right and wrong, good and bad, and nothing in between. Problems that are morally ambiguous, or those that require emotional tact, create difficulties for individuals and organizations that are lopsidedly analytically intelligent. In these settings, such individuals and organizations become more wedded to their black-and-white thinking and fixated on the outcomes of their analysis. The result is inflexibility in decision making.

Analysis Paralysis

When analytical agility is overemphasized at the cost of other agilities, individuals and organizations get too trapped in admiring the elegance of problem solving and the continual tweaking of analysis to see the impact on outcomes. When challenged for the practical results of their analysis, they attempt to gather more data and information, and engage in more slicing and dicing of data. Captivated by the nitty-gritty of their analysis, they lose sight of the big picture. In the HBO documentary *Manhunt* (2013), which details the efforts of the CIA in tracking Osama bin Laden to his hideout in Abbottabad in Pakistan, the brilliant analyst Nada Bakos says, "Fantastic analysts have patience and perseverance. And [they're] not always looking for the sexy payoff immediately." Such analysts do not suffer from analysis paralysis.

Defensiveness

Since analytical agility prides itself on the logic and rightness of its analysis and conclusions, it becomes argumentative and critical of others who question the analysis or want to use a method other than analysis to solve a problem. Creative solutions are viewed with suspicion and skepticism because they usually defy the traditionally accepted methods that analytical agility reveres. Operational solutions are condemned as the habits of fools who rush where angels fear to tread. Communicative solutions are deemed to have been proposed by people who talk through their hats. And visionary solutions are dismissed as soothsaying.

Overreliance on Analytical Agility: An Illustration

A little over twenty years after being founded, Enron had become America's seventh-largest company. For six years in a row, *Fortune* magazine ranked it as the Most Innovative Company in America; it was the darling of Wall Street, which both admired Enron and was terrified of it; Enron was the company that people dreamed of working for. In 2000, Enron reported that its profits increased by 45 percent, to $919 million, and its revenues doubled to $60 billion. And then, suddenly, a few months later, in the second half of 2001, as its dark story unraveled, Enron crashed to the ground, burning and destroying in the process the lives of many others. No phoenix would rise from these ashes. One executive killed himself, others saw their reputations dragged into the mud, and many investors—small and big—were ruined financially.

The story of Enron is a sordid saga in the history of business. It is also a tragic account of analytical agility that went berserk, unchecked. This story has been recounted and analyzed too many times now, most lucidly in *The Smartest Guys in the Room*.[19] So I will not engage in any analysis of Enron's fall. What is important for us to recognize is that Enron is a classic—even if stark—illustration of how things can unfold when people and organizations rely only on analytical agility without paying attention to whether the context requires its use. Jeff Skilling, the brilliant Harvard MBA and ex–McKinsey consultant, built, as CEO of Enron, a team around smart management graduates and McKinsey alums like himself.[20] He epitomized the prioritization of analytical agility at the expense of every other kind of agility, especially visionary agility.

The Smartest Guys describes Skilling as becoming such an influence in the company because of his "particular brand of agility," which built almost exclusively on analytical agility: "When people describe Skilling they don't just use the word 'smart'; they use phrases like 'incandescently brilliant' or 'the smartest person I ever met.' Skilling in the late 1980s wasn't a physically striking man—he was smallish, a little pudgy, and balding—but his mental agility was breathtaking. He could process information and conceptualize new ideas with blazing speed. He could instantly simplify highly complex issues into a sparkling, compelling image."[21]

But at the same time, Skilling had terrible flaws. He

had very poor management skills. He displayed a significant lack of communicative agility—he didn't know how to work with people and had nothing but contempt for people who didn't think like him. He suffered from a lack of operational agility too. He never got down to operational details and had an active dislike for the messy nitty-gritty of implementing an idea. An Enron executive described him as a "designer of ditches, not a digger of ditches." And of course the very fact that he used his brilliance to create the mirage of a successful company around a model that held no water, with no care for ethics or the plight of Enron's stockholders, shows he singularly lacked visionary agility.

Jeff Skilling epitomized the culture of Enron. Many senior executives at Enron—Andrew Fastow, the CFO, for instance—emulated Skilling because the corporate culture rewarded people who prioritized analytical agility at the expense of the other agilities. And so Enron became ridiculously lopsided in its use of analytical agility. It paid the price, but unfortunately so did Enron shareholders, many of whom lost their life savings.

Chapter 4

Operational Agility: Driving Leadership through Action

WITH MORE THAN FIFTY-SIX thousand species of plants, about seventeen hundred species of birds, and nearly two thousand species of animals, Brazil is one of the most biologically diverse regions of the world. Nearly 35 percent of the world's remaining rain forests are in Brazil, most of them in the Amazon basin, where that mighty river—the world's largest—discharges fifty-three million gallons into the ocean every second, and drains into an area spread over nine countries and covering about 40 percent of the South American continent (equivalent to nearly 90 percent of the area of the entire contiguous United States). This setting seems ideal to situate our story of leadership through operational agility. This story is complicated, however, because it is not just one of human enterprise versus the awesome power of nature; it is also a case where human intelligence is pitted against the wickedness of human nature with its propensity for greed and violence. Let me tell you the victorious story of Rosário Costa Cabral, a diminutive, illiterate woman who faced these odds and, in a classic illustration of operational agility, transformed her twenty-five-acre farm into an agricultural miracle and emerged as a leader in the field of sustainable agriculture.

Although Brazil is home to more than a third of the world's rain forests, the story of these rain forests is not a happy one. The statistics are especially shocking. The 2.5 million square miles of rain forest have seen remarkable levels of deforestation in recent decades. Forty years ago, only 2.4 percent of the Amazonian forest area had been lost; since the 1970s, however, the deforestation has extended to about 20 percent, and every year an additional 0.5 percent of forestland is lost.[22] A *National Geographic* article claims that in the time it would take to read that article, "an area of Brazil's rain forest larger than 200 football fields" would have been destroyed.[23]

Some of the deforestation has been in the name of progress. The twenty-five-hundred-mile Trans-Amazonian Highway (BR-230) accomplished more than its purpose of connecting parts of Brazil and its neighboring countries—it allowed easy access to the Amazonian forests and facilitated transportation of the vast amount of timber cut from huge tracts in the forests. Another paved highway, BR-163, called the "soy highway," runs through the forests for eleven hundred miles, neatly dividing the Amazon. On both sides of the highway, huge areas of the forests have been flattened into commercial soy fields as "legalized agriculturists" joined the ranks of bulldozer-equipped mining companies and chainsaw-bearing land-grabbers in ruthlessly exploiting the forest.

Beyond the three thousand miles of paved road these two highways offer, more than a hundred thousand miles of unauthorized roads branch off into the forests. Using these roads, timber poachers reach deep into the forest and illegally log and export mahogany and other hardwoods. Occasionally, crazes in the Western world create additional pressures on the rain forests—in the 1980s, for instance, growing demand in the United States for palm-heart salad led to armed gangs roaming the Amazonian waterways and indiscriminately killing the palm forests that lined the banks of the Amazon's tributaries. Gunmen, paid assassins, and mafia are now part of a volatile struggle for control over forestland with native populations that have lived there in ecologically friendly ways for centuries.

The deforestation, needless to say, has been ecologically devastating. Now, the high tides the river brings twice a day reach deeper into the forests, and at levels that are higher than in previous years. In spring, floods that engulf communities along the riverbanks are more widespread, and in the drier months the rainfall has decreased.

In this inhospitable context where nature and commercial interests combine in violent and destructive ways to thwart farming, Rosário Costa Cabral is pushing the boundaries of sustainable agriculture, equipped only with a small machete and a great deal of operational agility.

Quilombola *History*

Rosário—officially Maria do Rosário Costa Cabral—was born in 1950 in a small poverty-stricken community in the Amazon basin called Ipanema. She belongs to a *quilombola* community. These communities were thought to have been "lost" or "destroyed" until they became exposed with the recent deforestation and deeper forays of "civilization" into the Brazilian forests. And as they have emerged from oblivion, they have had to fight for rights to the lands they have lived on and cultivated for centuries.

The story of the *quilombolas* goes back four hundred years to the time when the Europeans discovered the New World. Christopher Columbus's voyage to the Caribbean began Europe's sustained contact and exploitation of South America. As the Europeans found vast expanses of land to cultivate and thick forests to tame, they sought the labor they needed but did not have. Thus began the transatlantic slave trade in which millions of people from West Africa were captured and brought to the Americas. It is estimated that for every white immigrant to the Americas there were four black immigrants. From the early sixteenth century to the late nineteenth century, English, Italian, and Spanish ships deposited nearly 10.5 million abducted West Africans as slaves along the eastern coastline of the two Americas, from New England in the north to Cape Horn in the south.[24] Nearly 1.5 million more died while being transported across the Atlantic.

Brazil was not just the geographic center of this long, two-continent coastline; it was also the primary customer of the slave trade—approximately 40 percent of the abducted Africans were brought to Brazil. For every African slave taken to North America, twelve slaves landed in Brazil. The sugarcane plantations and gold mines called for extremely hard labor in tropical climates, and many of the Africans ran away into the unknown jungles, preferring to face wild animals and dangerous native tribes rather than the slave drivers. This led to communities of Africans—known by the oxymoronic term "free slaves"—populating the Brazilian forests. There they mixed with the indigenous Americans, forming settlements called *quilombos*. And this is where we see a remarkable aspect of this otherwise sordid story: the *quilombolas* (the residents of the *quilombos*) developed a wonderful mixture of African, indigenous American, and sometimes European agricultural techniques as they farmed the forests. For instance, using African know-how, they made metal farming implements; they adopted the local production techniques that mixed cereal crops (corn, rice, and various native cereals) and forest produce like palms and papayas.

A Twenty-Five-Acre
Salt-Water-Flooded Farm

Rosário's family has constantly struggled in a practical and hard-hitting way. Her father was a rubber tapper whose meager earnings supported a family that included Rosário and her brothers. Without the ability to obtain or show titles to the lands they cultivated, the family, like most *quilombolas*, set up farms many times, only to be evicted by commercial interests, the mafia, the government, or a combination of them. The family moved across the land, surviving by selling the shrimp, fruit, and tree oils they harvested from the wild forest. Thus when the opportunity arose, in 1991, to buy twenty-five acres of land along one of the Amazon's tributaries, Rosário and her brothers grabbed it. It wasn't much of a farm. Located in the midst of a maze of small tributaries, the farm was flooded twice a day by tides. The mud was thick and gooey, making it difficult to walk, let alone farm. And excessive logging had left the land barren.

Transformation through Operational Agility

Over the years, Rosário has transformed this parcel of land into what today looks like virgin tropical forestland: there are tall trees and rich vines, waterways follow their natural courses through the farm, and the soil is fertile with leaves and mulch from the trees, just as it is in the untouched Amazonian forest.

In a classic demonstration of operational agility, Rosário selected and nurtured virtually every species seen today on her farm—almost nothing has grown by itself. She worked on the farm using techniques passed on by her father, drawing on knowledge built over the centuries as African and indigenous American cultures came together. Immediately after purchasing the land, she planted fast-growing timber trees that she could supply to local mills, and thus earn good money quickly. The crops traditionally grown in the delta could no longer be grown in the flooded forest. So Rosário experimented with new crops and techniques, learning through trial and error.

Her success with cassava, whose starchy root is a staple across most of South America, remarkably illustrates operational agility in practice. Cassava roots are a rich source of carbohydrates; the dried extract looks like small pearls and is called tapioca. She seeded her cassava garden with hardy seeds she had brought from her previous farms. She chose to begin the planting in November, when the tides are low and when the seedlings would find a more hospitable environment. For two years, as she planted, she studied the patterns: How far into her farm did the salt water flood? How deep was it? Which plant species survived at what depth? Rosário assessed the salt tolerance and hardiness of various species—cassava, for instance, could take up to two feet of flooding, she discovered. Following this, she bred more generations of the same plants and seeds, exploiting the plants' natural ability to adapt to obtain hardier and stronger plants in succeeding generations.

Today, after a little over two decades of farming, Rosário and her brothers grow hundreds of forest products—fruits like coconut, guava, banana, lime, and the antioxidant-rich açai berry and local produce like alligator cacao, cassava, and pineapple, which she has started growing at the base of her açai trees. Displaying a native understanding of supply-and-demand economics, she hedges her bets by growing a diverse portfolio of plants and trees. For instance, the farm grows hardwood tree varieties that are fast-growing and provide timber quickly, but there are also some that take two hundred years to mature.

Instead of treating the salt water as an enemy, Rosário exploits the tides that come twice a day by running a saltwater farm that cultivates shrimp and dozens of varieties of fish. She uses the forest undergrowth to create a naturally bounded nursery, and has planted trees whose fruits fall and attract fish into the saltwater farm. She uses woven traps—identical, incidentally, to those used in West Africa—to catch shrimp, and the farm harvests nearly sixty-six pounds of shrimp a week, providing food for the family apart from earning money in the market. Demonstrating an intelligence that creates flexibility in the supply chain, she has built cold-storage facilities so she can sell her produce and seafood only when market prices are high.

Miguel Pinedo-Vasquez, an ecologist from Columbia University, calls Rosário "a master of adaptation."[25] Rosário has achieved all this primarily by using operational agility. Most important of all, however, is that she has emerged as a leader in her community. She is generous with her knowledge—she distributes her hardy salt-water-resistant tubers and seeds to others in the community and shares with them what she has learned from her operations.

Operational Intelligence and Operational Agility

Operational intelligence drives agility that is action oriented—imagine a general leading his troops from the front, a coach demonstrating how to hold a tennis racquet, a company adjusting its server capabilities to meet a sudden increase in demand, or a manufacturing facility finding ways to continue production when a machine has failed. All these are examples of operational agility, where the flexibility is situated in an ability to respond to an emergent situation through hands-on action. The impact of operational agility can sometimes be dramatic and lifesaving. As we saw in the example of Nokia, its tremendous supply chain agility helped it not only to overcome the negative impacts of a fire in its supplier's factory but to also outlast com-

Operational agility helps people and organizations find alternative ways to do things when the routine or traditional practice breaks down.

petition. Operational agility helps people and organizations find alternative ways to do things when the routine or traditional practice breaks down.

Let's take a look at some specific types of agilities that operational intelligence brings to organizations.

Product Agility

In April 2009 technicians at the Naval Health Research Center in San Diego tested a swab from a nine-year-old girl for the flu virus. They discovered a flu strain they had never seen before. They classified it as an "unsubtypable" influenza A, but soon, as it spread rapidly across the world, it came to be known commonly as "swine flu." Millions of people were affected by the swine flu epidemic, and an estimated 203,000 people died. In the thick of this, vaccine producers like GlaxoSmithKline and Sanofi-Aventis were challenged. They had to find ways to quickly switch from making regular flu vaccine to producing the swine-flu vaccine. The ability to meet such a sudden demand for a product different from what you are making is what I call *product agility*. Customer service agents demonstrate similar product agility when they are able to service and sell multiple products or services, seamlessly shifting between them.

Input Agility

We may have to work with inputs of a nature or quality that is different from the one our production process normally uses. A person or company with *input agility* is able to speedily produce a good or service of equivalent quality even though using a new or different set of inputs. The CEO of World, the fashion apparel company headquartered in Kobe, Japan, realized that if a particular design is selling well but it's run out of buttons, employing regular processes to decide on a substitute can be very slow: "The season will end by the time you make a decision."[26] Thus, World's teams are empowered to make a wide range of decisions about production and design *without consulting their bosses*, and this drives World's operational agility. It is significant to remember, as this example illustrates, that operational agility is achieved not only through machines and computers; in fact, operational agility is achieved through the drive of *people* as often as it is through the flexibility of machines.

Process Agility

You have a critical meeting with a client tomorrow, and the point person on your team calls in sick. Can you find an alternate person who can step in to handle the meeting? Or you receive a phone call telling you that your company's credit card operations are stalled because of a computer glitch. Can you find another way of handling payments? If you have *process agility*, you can find alternative ways of doing things when a crisis comes up.

Scale Agility

Operational agility enables a company to recognize when production has to be scaled up or down and offers methods to achieve that dynamic scaling. This is called *scale agility* or *volume agility*. People or organizations that are able to scale dynamically can adjust to vagaries of market demand. It's important to note that in manufacturing contexts, scale agility is not necessarily located in the production process—sometimes the supply chain can offer storage space for work in progress or finished goods—this storage capability can provide the ability to scale up or down to meet demand by using its buffer stock.

What Operational Agility Does

As we've seen, operational agility drives leadership through action—the individual or the company responds to change by resorting to dynamic action rather than to the contemplative thinking associated with analytical agility or to the verbal dexterity associated with communicative agility. Operational agility gives expression to the leader's will and determination—actions convey the leader's courage, strength, and purpose. An operationally intelligent leader is easy to spot: she or he is focused on making decisions and achieving results. This is sometimes exemplified by a military officer, who is tough and quick in decision making, and bold to take actions that others would be afraid to take.

At the same time, someone like Rosário Costa Cabral is also the epitome of operational agility. As we saw from her story, her first response was action; she then observed the effects of her actions and modified them using what she had learned from her observations. Whether it is a military officer or a gentle farmer, action is central to operational agility.

Used properly, operational agility transforms ideas into reality, knowing into doing. Inventive agility (as we will see in the next chapter) may generate a creative idea, but for the idea to see the light of day, operational agility is needed—to produce the prototype, take it through production, and bring it into the market. Analytical agility may result in a list of the pros and cons of different kinds of conceptual methods, but operational agility cuts a practical path through the theory jungle. Communicative agility may talk the talk, but operational agility walks the walk.

> *Operational agility transforms ideas into reality, knowing into doing.*

Where Can You Use Operational Agility?

Operational agility is the primary skill set needed in leadership situations that call for action. It requires individuals and companies to demonstrate leadership through example. When hard decisions have to be made, it is operational agility that comes to the fore. For example, when a decisive action is needed to commit to a new project, or to end an existing project, operational agility becomes very helpful. If operational agility is used well, project creep—the tendency to let projects that are clearly failing continue under one pretext or another—can be dramatically reduced.

The Case of Zara

Amancio Ortega started Inditex, a small clothes-manufacturing company, in 1963, choosing to locate it in A Coruña, a midsized port city in the extreme northwest of Spain. In 1975, Inditex faced a critical test—a German wholesaler canceled a large order and Ortega was left with a huge pile of finished clothes. He had invested all his capital in this order and now had no large buyers. He decided to sell them himself by setting up a store. He wanted to call the store Zorba, after *Zorba the Greek*, but a local bar called Zorba protested. Ortega then decided to name the store Zara, using the letter molds that he had already made for Zorba.[27]

Today, Amancio Ortega is the third-richest person in the world; Inditex is a $22 billion company that has eight recognized brands across the world, the main one being Zara, which often stands in as the name for Inditex. (As is common practice, I will use Zara in this discussion to refer to the Inditex group.) Zara has nearly sixty-five hundred stores in eighty-eight markets across the world and employs more than 128,000 people. But size is not the secret behind Zara's success; rather, it is agility—and particularly operational agility. We get a hint from the company website, which says, "A state of the art logistics system centered in Spain helps deliver new products to all of the Group's stores twice weekly to meet our customers' needs." In fact, customer centricity drives the operational agility, and that in turn drives Zara's growth. And the growth is striking—in 2013 alone, across its eight brands, Zara entered thirty new markets across the world.

Zara's business model is focused on fast fashion—the ability to spot emerging customer needs or preferences in fashion and to quickly meet those emerging demands. According to Zara's chairman José María Castellano, "This business is all about reducing response time. In fashion, stock is like food. It goes bad quick."[28] Such an assessment makes three demands on Zara from a sense-and-respond perspective:

1. The company needs to be able to sense market trends quickly and accurately.
2. The company needs to design and create new products quickly.
3. The supply chain must be agile so it can get the finished products to the customers quickly.

Sensing Market Trends

Most clothing companies spend a lot of time and effort trying to predict what the next season's trend will be. They do this in various ways: through a committee of market observers that votes on styles and fashions for the next year; through sophisticated forecasting mechanisms that project trends based on various demographic characteristics and business data; and through trade shows where retailers, via early purchasing decisions, reveal the trends they anticipate in the coming months or year. Using this information, designers spend the next few months creating physical samples, assembling a product portfolio, developing cost models, planning production, and ultimately outsourcing the actual production in large lot sizes to producers in various countries where there are significant cost savings. The entire process from trend forecasting to actual production may take upward of a year, and because of supply chain sluggishness, it may take several months to fulfill orders from retailers.

Zara overturns this model. Instead of relying on theoretical or expert-based assessments of what will sell, it actually puts its ears to the ground and its eyes on the store shelves. Like any responsive company in the retail business, it gets point of sale (POS) data every evening from its retailers—the POS data gives it a good idea of what is selling and what inventory is left in the stores. But Zara goes beyond POS—it gets to know *what would have sold* and *what customers would have liked.* This information comes to it from its store associates who talk to customers. Why didn't they buy the dress they tried? What did they not like: The floral pattern? The color? The buttons? Or the design itself? In an *upward chain of information,* such information flows from the associates through the store manager to the company headquarters in Spain. This, of course, demonstrates a core belief for Zara to remain "focused on listening closely to its customers to offer them the fashions they desire." But more important than that is what Zara does *after* listening— Zara delivers to customers what they want, and it achieves this through its design and manufacturing processes, which I will describe in the next section.

Zara does another thing very differently—through its manufacturing process, it also dictates to the customer what he or she should buy. It manufactures products in small lots and supplies them to its stores in smaller lots. Customers are told that the products available for sale in the store are constantly changing, and that styles and products *change* twice a week—they are not replenished. In other words, if you like what you see, grab it now. Do not wait until next week—it may be gone by then. This enables Zara to move away from two related practices that have become standard in the industry: it does not have to manage inventories and supply chains created by long product life cycles, and it does not have to hold markdown sales to get rid of unsold inventories. This has a significant impact on the bottom line: Zara's gross profit margins (GPMs) are 15–20 percent higher than the GPMs of other apparel manufacturers (for instance, over the last five years Gap has averaged a GPM of 39.4 percent, while Zara has had an average GPM of 56.5 percent).[29]

Designing, Manufacturing, and Supplying Products Quickly

Zara can take inputs from its stores, create a design, turn it into a product, and have it on its store shelves within two weeks. Tommy Hilfiger rather disparagingly called Zara's products "disposable fashion" recently but was quick to admit that that's the ruling style for the moment.[30] One of the key takeaways Zara has identified is that if you want speed, you cannot allow gaps between design and production. Zara's designers sit *in* the production process, and there are three lines—men's, women's, and children's—which often duplicate resources in order to achieve speed and both gender- and age-specific specialty of design. Based on the design trends that are emerging from the stores, three groups—designers (who conceptualize the new product), commercial managers (who know the market), and procurement and production managers (who understand the manufacturing process) work together to determine design elements—the cut, the look and feel, the fabric to be used, the manufacturing details, the cost, and the price. A sketch is made and a prototype is assembled. Small prototype workshops are located amidst them so they can see and comment on products as they emerge, and any necessary modifications can be made quickly.

Interestingly, the "new" design typically modifies or extends a current design—using existing style elements and fabric and trim already available in Zara's warehouse makes the process move quickly. Approvals are easy because designers, commercial managers, and production engineers are all working in the same location. The result is a superfast design process. In fact, Zara's speed in design comes from most of its innovation being incremental, not radical. Zara has been accused of stealing designs from famous fashion designers and modifying them just enough to avoid potential lawsuits. Masoud Golsorkhi, editor of *Tank*, a London fashion magazine, says, "To the luxury brands, they [Zara] are copycats, they are like mushrooms feeding off the main body of fashion. . . . I was of the same mind myself, but I have grown out of that because I realize that the fashion companies also copy each other. In the end, no one's original."[31]

Zara's agility can be traced to an intelligence-driven mind-set that is a clean break from Taylorian mind-sets that focus on economy and efficiency. In keeping with the intelligence-driven approach, Zara does some things that would be considered contrarian in the fashion industry. First, it chooses to produce mostly in Spain. More than 50 percent of Zara's production is local, although labor costs in Spain are about five to six times higher than in China or India. In fact, rather than follow the practice of apparel manufacturers who seek to drive down production costs by manufacturing in countries like the Dominican Republic or Bangladesh, where labor is cheap, Zara chooses to produce in assembly workshops—mostly outsourced—located within a few miles of its corporate headquarters. This allows the company tremendous speed, flexibility, and accuracy in the design-to-production process.

Second, while "lean manufacturing" is the mantra in most companies, Zara, as we saw in the description of the design process, deliberately duplicates resources. It has three separate lines—men's, women's, and children's—which means that Zara's factories have excess capacities; in fact, as much as 40 percent excess capacity. Zara uses these excess capacities to easily meet sudden surges in demand or to work with unforeseen design or production deadlines.

Third, production lot sizes are not focused on economies of scale; rather, they focus on agility—small lot sizes prevent long-term commitment to fashion trends that turn out to be fickle and short-lived. In this way, while other apparel manufacturers are governed by market demands stemming from a fickle fashion customer, Zara actually leads the customer into buying patterns.

Fourth, Zara produces a large variety of products, although its production runs are small. This provides it another kind of hedge against uncertain customer demand—if a product is selling out, there is a variant that a customer may find to be close enough to substitute for the sold-out product. As a *Harvard Business Review* article points out, "Empty racks at Zara don't drive customers to other stores. Being out of stock in one item helps sell another."[32]

Fifth and finally, Zara recognizes that the common base material in all its products is unbleached cloth. Now, procuring this cloth takes a long time, because it has to be sourced from international markets. Delays in supply could be fatal to a particular fashion line. Zara therefore buys and stores large quantities of partly unfinished semicolored or uncolored fabric that it can color and use according to the demands it sees in the market.

> *"You need to have five fingers touching the factory and five touching the customer."*

Amancio Ortega learned an early lesson from the crisis that made him open the first Zara store in 1975: "You need to have five fingers touching the factory and five touching the customer." Zara has built its tremendous success by implementing that lesson—powered primarily by operational agility.

The Downside of Excessive Operational Agility

As I discussed in the previous chapter, every agility has some negative characteristics associated with it if it is left to run unchecked at the expense of the other agilities. When operational agility runs amok, it creates many problems.

Micromanagement

Since operational agility is very action oriented, when it is in excess you will have a tendency to want to get involved in everything and to control everything that is going on.

Excessive operational agility creates helicopter parents and Big Brother bosses who are constantly looking over the shoulders of their wards and subordinates. When overexercised, operational agility does not allow you to delegate work—your subordinates are expected to measure and report so many things that it stifles independence and thwarts innovation. Contrary to its promise, unbridled operational agility ends up *lowering* efficiency and productivity.

> *Excessive operational agility creates helicopter parents and Big Brother bosses.*

Undirected Action for Action's Sake

Since operational agility helps in solving problems by taking action, when you have it in excess, you become convinced that you have to be running around and doing things—something, anything. That, you will think, is better than engaging in reflection or imagination, which, of course, is "doing nothing." You will operate with all the purposefulness of a headless chicken. If it is ungoverned, operational agility can transform you into Lewis Carroll's Red Queen, who grabs Alice's hand and runs and runs, to get nowhere.

Intimidation

Since operational agility measures success by how much action is being taken, it can create win-or-lose attitudes and insensitive styles of working. When you jump in to do everything that everybody else is doing, it creates a sense of intimidation and an atmosphere of fear. The Red Queen in *Through the Looking-Glass* morphs into the strict Queen of Hearts in *Alice's Adventures in Wonderland*. And the Queen of Hearts, you may remember, created an atmosphere of fear in Wonderland: "The Queen had only one way of settling all difficulties, great or small. 'Off with his head!' she said, without even looking round."

Thus an overreliance on operational agility can have drastic and dramatic consequences on companies and individuals. As we saw earlier in this book, Nokia, despite tremendous supply chain flexibility, ultimately had to exit the mobile phone market because it lacked the communicative agility to sense customer needs, and the visionary agility to chart the future of the operating system its phones used.

Chapter 5

Inventive Agility: Finding Creative Solutions When You Need Them Most

T HE FLOW OF THE KĀVERI, the great river of South India, is arrested at Tiruchirappalli in the state of Tamil Nadu by a stone dam built by the Chola kings in the second century CE. In Tamil, the local language, the two-thousand-year-old dam is called Kallanai (combining *kallu*, "stone," and *anai*, "dam"), but it is more popularly known by the name the British colonizers gave it: the Grand Anicut. The word "anicut" is perhaps a corrupted combination of two Tamil words—*anai* and *kattu* (build)—designed to roll easily off English tongues.

However, the anicut is not technically a dam but a stone weir. Weirs are rather low structures that are built across rivers not so much to stop their flow but more to break them into multiple streams that are manageable from the perspective of irrigation and also, often, to prevent the river from flooding. The Grand Anicut, in particular, is an eighteen-foot-high wall that is ninety-five feet long and sixty-six feet wide. It separates the Kāveri into four streams: Kollidam Aru, Puthu Aru, Vennaru, and Kaviri.

Although the Grand Anicut was built many centuries ago, our story begins much later. In 1827 a twenty-four-year-old British engineer, Arthur T. Cotton, was charged with the task of inspecting the Grand Anicut. The young engineer recommended some minor but urgent repairs to the structure. The British government of Madras, however, dragged its feet. It did not do anything until 1830, when, ironically, Arthur Cotton himself, and his younger brother and assistant Frederick Cotton, also an engineer, were again tasked with examining the anicut. Following this second inspection, the Cottons were commissioned to cut sluices in the Grand Anicut through which the silt sediment that had built up over the centuries would flow out.

The Madras School of Engineering: Two-Thousand-Year-Old Lessons in Frugal Innovation

Lady Hope, Arthur Cotton's daughter, recounts a memorable event in her biography of her father. Upon cutting into the Grand Anicut, Frederick Cotton discovered a strange fact. To his amazement, he found that the anicut was not—despite its name—a stone wall at all. Rather, it "was hardly more than a mass of rubbish, mud, stones, and logs of wood, the safety of which depended solely on its then plastered surface."[33] As Bret Wallach, a cultural geographer and professor at the University of Oklahoma, sums up: "It was an important, perhaps even a revolutionary discovery: simple inertia had been great enough to withstand sixteen hundred annual floods."[34]

For Arthur and Frederick Cotton, this discovery gave rise to what they termed the Madras, or "cheap School of Engineering"[35]—a model of frugal innovation that the Chola kings had built almost two thousand years before the term was reinvented with its modern fad status among management theorists.

After the Grand Anicut cleaning was completed, Arthur Cotton's next project was to build the Coleroon Anicut, slightly downstream across the Kāveri (Coleroon was the anglicized name for Kollidam). Here Cotton applied what he had learned from the Grand Anicut: instead of a grand European-style dam, he replicated the minimalist approach of the Cholas. And we can say that he had learned the lesson well, for the Coleroon Anicut stands even today, irrigating a vast tract of about half a million acres, a shining example of the Madras cheap School of Engineering.

Emboldened by his experience at replicating the design of the Grand Anicut in his work on the Coleroon Anicut, Arthur Cotton used the same minimalist, resource-savvy design in a tremendously ambitious project elsewhere—to control the "greatest river of South India"—the Godavari.

The Godavari is the second-largest river in India (after the Ganga). It starts in the western mountains in the state of Maharashtra and runs southeast for roughly nine hundred miles across the Deccan Plateau, through the states of Andhra Pradesh and Telangana, and empties itself into the Bay of Bengal on the east coast of India. Its basin extends across nearly 121,000 square miles. Before joining the sea, the river divides into two at a city called Rajahmundry and forms a large delta. The British estimate of the river's discharge should tell you something about its size: the discharge of the Godavari was three times that of the Nile and more than two hundred times the water of the Thames.

Until about the mid-nineteenth century, ironically, the areas through which the mighty Godavari flowed were destitute. With no structures to harness the river, it often flooded the region. And the loss of food crops caused repeated famines. In addition, the region, which cultivated cotton in its rich black soil, was facing severe competition from the cotton factories of Manchester. Consequently, farmers in the region were poverty-stricken and virtually hopeless.

Arthur Cotton, following his experience with the Grand Anicut and the Coleroon Anicut, proposed to the British government that a major project be undertaken to tame the mighty Godavari. And thus, in 1847, Arthur Cotton was commissioned to build a dam across the river. Cotton chose a spot close to the village of Dowleswaram, where the river is approximately four miles wide but is broken by three islands that together cover about a mile. The Godavari Anicut, also called the Dowleswaram Barrage, was completed in 1852 as four twelve-foot-high anicuts that span about three miles and irrigate a million acres. The success of the project can be seen in the effect it has had over the last century—an impoverished, famine-struck area has been transformed into a resource-rich and prosperous region. In fact, it is now one of the wealthiest regions of India.

Arthur Cotton embodies *inventive agility*—he picked

up a lesson in invention from two millennia ago and put it into practice to solve a contemporary problem. Using the same principles as the Chola engineers of the second century CE, he built the four anicuts across the Godavari, not as solid masses of masonry, but as stone coatings over the sand of the riverbed. As Frederick Cotton wrote of his brother: "And, after all, what is good engineering but economy! Any engineer can do anything with money; the question is how to do great things at little cost."[36]

Inventive Intelligence and Inventive Agility

The story of Sir Arthur Cotton and the construction of the Coleroon and Godavari anicuts in nineteenth-century India provides a remarkable illustration of the use and the impact of inventive agility. Inventive agility, as its name obviously indicates, becomes necessary when a problem requires a creative, nontraditional solution. It becomes particularly apparent when a leader or a company draws lessons from one context and applies them to another.

While operational agility drives the process of adaptation as it makes changes to scale and scope in accordance with the environment, inventive agility drives innovation, often resorting to an alternative process of *exaptation*—

an evolutionary process by which biological organisms find alternative uses for features they already possess.

A classic example of this is birds: feathers originally evolved to help birds fly, but over millennia they became useful in regulating body temperature too. The connection of exaptation to intelligence (and hence to agility) is brought out by a simple unconscious act that we often execute in our daily lives: if we need to change a light-bulb and do not have a stepladder, we use a chair. The chair is designed to sit on, but of course it can be used as a stepladder. In extending the parallel to innovation, exaptation may create new uses for a product either in the same market or in different markets.

To give you an example: Philips sold a soy-milk maker in China, and when it discovered the market for soup makers in France, it quickly adapted the same machine for the French market. Philips then took a lesson in innovation from that and is now exploring how to convert a rice cooker into a spiced-biryani maker for the Indian market.

What Inventive Agility Does

Inventive agility provides tremendous advantages to the leader or the agile organization. Among others, three critical roles of inventive agility are its ability to provide broad systemic perspectives, its ability to challenge the status quo and established dogmas, and its ability to complement the analytical and operational agilities.

Provides Broad Systemic Perspectives

Inventive agility is most useful in discerning the uniqueness of individual phenomena and using this knowledge to make connections and establish interrelationships between diverse phenomena. Since creative insight comes mostly from perceiving the everyday world, inventive agility is critically involved in transforming sensory experience into deep insight.

Challenges the Status Quo

Inventive intelligence and inventive agility drive that flash of creative insight that combines seemingly unrelated phenomena in ingeniously productive ways. Analytical agility is concerned with the question, *Why?* Operational agility is concerned with, *How?* But inventive agility is centered on the question, *Why not?* Thus a person or organization possessing high inventive agility is able to quickly think of solutions that challenge established orthodoxy with out-of-the-box perspectives.

Enhances Analytical and Operational Agilities

Inventive agility enhances the analytical agility of an agile leader or organization—as analytical agility tries to resolve ambiguity through analysis, inventive agility helps to connect the dots and see patterns that enable analysis and judgment. In conjunction with operational agility, inventive agility is able to visualize the practical details in implementing ideas and to adopt an appropriate course of action for a given situation.

Shakes up the Organization

Inventive agility is essential when creative solutions are needed, or when the status quo needs to be rattled. Given its ability to deal with ambiguity, inventive agility assists in handling situations in which there are no clear-cut data or solutions and there need to be a lot of experimental forays and then judgments based on the results of those experiments. Finally, inventive agility is needed whenever it is necessary to see the forest rather than the trees—larger contexts and connections become visible with this skill set, which may add value to analysis and operations that have been taking more limited perspectives.

Grace Manufacturing

If there is an epitome of a company that has survived and thrived because of inventive agility, it is a three-hundred-employee-strong company called Grace Manufacturing.[37] Richard Grace established the company in 1966, in Michigan, as a contract manufacturer of intricately etched metal parts. In 1977 he moved his company to the warmer climate of Russellville, Arkansas, where it is now headquartered, with a manufacturing plant in Mexico.

Grace Manufacturing had a proprietary process for making precise steel shapes, for which it was awarded a US patent in 1992. This process, called photochemical etching, gave Grace the ability to create intricate raised or recessed designs on the metal by removing thin layers of it using chemicals like ferric chloride, a corrosive compound. Thus, without metal burns or mechanical distortions from bending and shaping, Grace could create thin metal components that its customers used wherever there was a need for precisely shaped metal parts. One of Grace's key markets turned out to be the computer peripherals industry, especially the early dot matrix printer industry, for which Grace manufactured printer bands and heads.

In the 1970s, however, as printer technology began to change and dot matrix printers began to evolve, this major market for Grace's precisely shaped metal components began to disappear. When Grace realized its cash-cow business was under threat, it started to look for other markets for its products. In a stroke of inventive agility, Richard Grace and his children, Chris (now CEO) and Maria, recognized that one of the inadvertent side effects of their manufacturing process could become a competitive advantage: the razor-sharp steel edges that were created by photochemical etching. As Chris Grace recounts, "Back then, if you worked in the plant, it wasn't a question of whether you were going to cut your finger, but when. It got to be that, on the way to the Band-Aid station, you'd see a drop of blood every five feet." The inventive agility of the Graces was in recognizing that the ability to create these sharp edges could be of immense business value. "We realized we were good at making sharp things. And so we thought, what can we make that's sharp?" They thus created a line of woodworking tools, called Microplane, which included, for instance, "rotary shapers" that could be used for freehand contouring of wood, or handheld rasps, which allow for precise shaving of wooden parts.

In 1994, though, one of their dealers, Leonard and Lorraine Lee of Lee Valley Tools in Ottawa, Canada, discovered that the Microplane woodworking rasp could be used as a fabulous kitchen grater. Lorraine tried it out on an orange peel, and "lacy shards of zest fell from its surface like snowflakes."[38] Grace Manufacturing quickly made a few modifications to its design and created a whole new product line of must-have graters for cooks and chefs.

Instead of selling only a few rasps a month, sales of the Microplane graters rose to about ten thousand a year. Soon cooking instructors were promoting them in culinary classes, and today Microplane products dominate Grace's business, posting more than $20 million in annual sales. The company has continued to adapt the technology to other markets, such as medical products (a surgeon's tool to cut bone, for example) and cosmetics (a rasp to shave off foot calluses). Following the new ways customers use their products is important for Grace Manufacturing. For example, the senior management watches shows on the Food Network. "If your child was an actor, you'd watch for him," Chris Grace explains. "Same deal with us."

Shadow Traits of Inventive Agility

As with everything, an excessive dependence on inventive agility brings its own problems. Let's look at a few of the common pitfalls that accompany an overreliance on thinking outside the box.

Scattered Thinking

When inventive agility is overused, there is often a lack of focus and inattention to detail. Overactive inventive agility is constantly in search of new ideas, new domains, new possibilities, even before exhausting the potential of the opportunities in hand. In this search for newness, there is a tendency to overlook practical details or to ignore long-term implications. Such minds are like monkeys, jumping from idea to idea, never reveling in the complete exploration of any single idea. To be effective, inventive agility needs to be harnessed by the other agilities—especially operational, visionary, and analytical. As the examples later in this chapter will indicate, when inventive agility runs amok, without attention to operational agility, a company can create too many product lines that become difficult to manage in terms of inventory and supply chains. And when inventive agility is not balanced with analytical agility, a company can create products that may be profitable on their own but are actually harmful to the company because they cannibalize the profits from its other products.

Overcommitment

An inventively intelligent mind sees possibilities in everything, and so every project, and every idea, looks attractive. The ability to discriminate is essential, whether in assessing the financial feasibility of an idea on the table (analytical agility) or in understanding operational complications that make an idea impractical (operational agility). Overactive inventive agility makes it impossible to say no to new projects, in turn making the individual or the company take on too much work. Overcommitment creates stress, and leads to operational breakdowns and possible loss of reputation.

Impractical Dreaming

If you have hyperactive inventive agility, you're prone to making unrealistic assessments. For the creative mind, every situation is an exciting possibility, and every situation is equally likely to develop. As a result, you see the world through rose-tinted glasses, and everything looks lopsidedly optimistic. When reality hits, the individual or the company with excessive inventive agility is not prepared, and can't offer any explanation for why things did not work out as envisioned.

Overreliance on
Inventive Agility: Two Illustrations

The use of the five agilities in context-appropriate ways helps us understand that contemporary management theory's emphasis on disruptive innovation—as if it were a panacea for all company ills—has to be tempered. As one CEO said to me, "This craze about disruptive innovation—it is like asking me to replace the heart of my company with a defibrillator."

The experience of innovative companies like Toyota, which implements one hundred thousand new ideas in its cars every year, shows that a culture of innovation requires a constant stream of incremental innovation and perhaps once in a while a disruptive innovation. Gary Pisano at Harvard argues that "all the excitement about disruptive innovation has blinded us to one simple but irrefutable economic fact: The vast majority of profit from innovation does not come from the initial disruption; it comes from the stream of routine, or sustaining, innovations that accumulate for years (sometimes decades) afterward."[39] I want to give you two examples of highly innovative companies that nearly failed because of too much innovation.

Avery Dennison

Avery Dennison, the famous label-making company, is renowned for its innovative ideas. It has moved into product areas such as stick-on automotive trim and heat-transfer inks and stickers for T-shirts and other clothing. However, Avery was having a problem converting its many ideas into products. As the *Wall Street Journal* reported, "Schedules were slipping. Customers were chafing."[40]

Frustrated, the company brought in external consultants to solve the problem. What did the consultants find? They made an amazing discovery: "Avery was jamming too many new ideas into its product pipeline, without enough slack time to ensure that critical tasks stayed on schedule." The recommendation was, "Shrink the number of rollouts." Tim Bond, a senior executive at Avery, remarked that this gave them a much better handle on new product planning, keeping their capacity in mind. Echoing the classic refrain of those who have wrestled with process improvement and bottlenecks, he says, "Instead of killing ourselves on too many projects, we think we're able to move a smaller number through the system more rapidly." Michael George, the external consultant who diagnosed Avery's problem, concluded, "If a freeway is getting congested, do you load more cars onto the ramp in the hopes that people will go faster? Or should you try to take some cars off? That's what we're talking about."

LEGO

/////////////////////////

No company is a better example of suffering from the woes of uncontrolled inventive agility than LEGO, the Danish toy maker that needs no introduction across the world.

Ole Kirk Christiansen, who was trying to survive during the Great Depression, founded LEGO in 1932. The name is a combination of two Danish words, *leg* (play) and *godt* (well)—and indeed, over the eighty years of its existence, LEGO has helped the world to play well. Ever since the company was established, it has had at its heart the philosophy that "good play" not only is a catalyst for a child's creativity but can also make an impact on the creativity of the adult the child becomes.

LEGO came out during the period of the Great Depression with the mission to help parents bring happiness to their children. And in this mission, LEGO has been tremendously innovative over the decades. The move from wooden toys to injection-molded plastic ones in the late 1930s and the invention of its universally recognized patented plastic building block are but two examples of its innovative spirit. LEGO combined entertainment and education in an irresistible combination that drove its profits upward year after year.

Until the 1990s, that is. In 1988 the last patent on the plastic brick that was at the core of LEGO's business expired. At the same time, the advent of video games and hi-tech toys combined to push children's interests away from the "old-fashioned" LEGO bricks. The threat to LEGO was very clear and financially tangible. For the first time in its history, after growing at a double-digit rate for fifteen consecutive years, in 1993 LEGO's sales plateaued.

And thus LEGO decided to bet on a surge of disruptive innovation that it believed would help it break through this ugly patch. In this innovative frenzy, it introduced many new product lines. One for babies was called Primo; it experimented with new material for its products, and its new Znap line featured more flexible plastic. It aimed for niche markets, so a product line called Scala, for Barbie lovers, was introduced; and it attempted to incorporate hi-tech into its bricks—the CyberMaster line had programmable bricks that could be coded and controlled to create LEGO objects with interesting movements. David Robertson notes in his insightful book *Brick by Brick* that "from 1994 to 1998, LEGO tripled the number of new toys it produced, introducing an average of five major new product themes each year."[41]

Unfortunately, all these product lines failed. In 1998, LEGO posted the first loss in its history—$38 million. Like the lame kid whom the Pied Piper of Hamelin left behind, LEGO was in danger of being left behind in the merciless competition of the toy industry. To overcome this, it decided it had to be even more disruptive in its innovation. It teamed up with Hollywood to introduce character-themed LEGO. In 1999 it signed up first to make LEGO games featuring characters from George Lucas's *Star Wars* and Disney's *Winnie the Pooh*, and then in 2000 it developed theme-based games with *Harry Potter* characters.

The worst, however, was yet to come. Not only did these innovations not contribute to the company's revenues, but instead they drained the company's coffers even further. Oddly, LEGO didn't notice. It was engaged in so much disruptive innovation that it was at the point of disrupting LEGO itself. For instance, it created the LEGO digital experience, where you could go online and pick virtual LEGO pieces and build virtual things without the real LEGO blocks. This went on until 2003, when "LEGO's sparks of brilliance almost burned down the company . . . they almost went bankrupt because of the way they managed innovation."[42]

As LEGO was tottering, its first nonfamily CEO, Jørgen Vig Knudstorp, was brought in. He began to rehabilitate a company that had been drunk on innovation. One of the key things the new management discovered was that LEGO had clearly neglected analytical agility— it had very poor data on its product lines. For instance, it did not even know which products were profitable and which were not. When the management analyzed the sales data, it discovered that the themed product lines suffered from two problems. First, sales were seasonal. The themed products sold only when a movie of that theme—*Star Wars* or *Harry Potter*, for example—was released. Second, and more dangerously, LEGO had made its brand subservient, perhaps even relinquished it, to the Hollywood brand. This realization—an exercise of visionary agility—brought home the long-term damage the company was doing to itself.

From an operational perspective, unbridled innovation had created a logistical nightmare. Compare this: In 1994, sixty years after its founding, LEGO products had increased to about 4,000 elements, but in the next three years, by 1997, this had increased to 6,000 elements, and by 2004 it had exploded to 14,200. There were, for instance, eight different policemen, three different villains, and three different chefs. Worse, they had noninterchangeable parts—for instance, you could not put one head on another body. You can imagine the havoc this caused in manufacturing and supply chain management.

Within a year, the new management reduced the number of elements by 50 percent. LEGO harnessed its inventive agility with the appropriate use of other agilities. It started to exercise its analytical agility to discover patterns and trends; it employed visionary agility to recognize and correct the long-term damage to the brand; and it used operational agility to bring the implications of the production process to bear upon the company's inventions. Thus LEGO has, in the years since 2004, been able to recover its place in the toy industry. For the last five years, it has posted a healthy 24 percent growth in sales and a 40 percent increase in profits every year.

Even when your product encourages imaginative play without limits, your vision and business strategy require more than unbridled creativity. As the rise, fall, and re-ascendance of LEGO makes clear, success is built on more than one agility, and it is managed brick by brick.

Chapter 6

///

Communicative Agility: Solving Problems Together

How do you persuade a group of subordinates to embark on a mission that borders on the suicidal? And what if, to complicate matters, you and your subordinates are surrounded by gory scenes of death—men being blown to bits by large guns, flaming cannonballs landing all around, bayonets splitting the chests of fighting men? What if the situation is so bad that your commanding general himself wants to be taken away from the battle, saying he can have no more of this bloody scene?[43] In such a setting, how do you inspire your men to embark on a mission in which their death is almost certain?

This is the situation that Napoléon Bonaparte, a young unknown lieutenant from Corsica, found himself in when he was posted to Toulon, the fortified French port city on the Mediterranean coast. It was held by the British, and the French Republican army had seen months of ineffective siege. Several bloody attempts to retake the port had been repulsed by the English-Spanish collaboration. Napoléon was now captain of the artillery in this messy combination of futile siege and bloody aggression. He started to assemble cannons and men to attack Toulon, which the British had so fortified that the French called it Little Gibraltar.

Napoléon had under him sixty-four officers and sixteen hundred troops. He put that authority to good use and built eight batteries of guns in the last two weeks of November 1793. He soon had thirty-seven cannons and twenty-six mortars, an arsenal that presented a considerable threat to the Anglo-Spanish forces in Toulon. It is in this construction of the batteries that Napoléon presents us with an excellent demonstration of communicative intelligence and agility.

Tremendous courage was required to build a battery of guns under enemy fire—pathways had to be made to the positions where the guns were to be placed, ramparts had to be built, then the heavy guns, cannonballs, and cases of gunpowder had to be moved to those positions, along with enough buckets of water to sponge and cool the guns between rounds of firing.

But Napoléon was immensely successful in motivating his troops. It could have been considered a suicidal effort in general, but there was one position that posed the most significant challenge. Napoléon realized that this position was extremely critical to his efforts—it was on a nearby hill and would allow him maximum advantage in shooting at the British fleet in Toulon's harbor. However, it was also the most exposed of all the gun positions, which meant that the British ships could both see the battery and fire at it at will. Napoléon's senior officers were very skeptical that they would find volunteers to construct the battery at that position, let alone man the guns there.

In a stroke of communicative genius, Napoléon realized that the secret to getting volunteers lay in the gun battery's name—he decided to call this position *La batterie des hommes sans peur* (The Battery of Men without Fear). He made his soldiers place a huge placard with that name over the battery's entrance. He made a speech to his artillery troops: "I need men, real men, men with balls, certainly not sissies. I would never ask them to take an enemy position, but I insist that they follow me to that position. If you are one of those men, raise your hand."[44] They all raised their hands and shouted, "Vive Bonaparte!" Following this direct appeal to every soldier's manhood and military identity—which are characterized by fearlessness—Napoléon never lacked soldiers willing to volunteer for that position; indeed, it became one of the most sought-after postings.[45]

It is worth noting that Napoléon communicated and inspired his men nonverbally too. We see a hint of this in his statement above, when he says he will not ask his soldiers "to take an enemy position," but he will need them to "follow" him to that position. In fact, he was perhaps the only commander who slept alongside his troops at the batteries—and, naturally, a tremendous sense of respect and loyalty developed among his soldiers toward him. Paintings and narratives of the time depict him standing prominently on the ramparts of the gun batteries in full sight of his enemies, taunting them to fire at him.

In a superhuman effort, Napoléon relentlessly pounded Toulon and its harbor for twenty hours a day, day after day.[46] On December 18, 1793, Napoléon led a fierce takeover of a critical British-held position called Fort Mulgrave, although he was wounded in the leg by a saber during the fight. His men put up a battery quickly, and soon they were raining terrifying cannonballs on the British fleet. Admiral Hood, the commanding officer of the Anglo-Spanish forces, ordered British withdrawal from Toulon. Napoléon was promoted to brigadier general, and thus began the climb to his ultimate success as emperor of France.[47]

Communicative Agility

Through communicative agility, you are adept at persuading others to do the "right" things. With this essential skill set, you convey empathy, sensitivity, and concern, and as a result, you generate such confidence and trust in others that, as in the case of Napoléon, they are even willing to lay down their lives for you. Communicative agility allows you to build and sustain relationships, even when times get tough. People with a high level of communicative agility focus on collaboration and togetherness, and create a joint sense of purpose by setting common goals designed for long-term success.

After all this talk of collaboration and working with others, you'll be wondering whether *emotional agility* fits here. Yes, emotional agility is part of communicative agility. But communicative agility goes beyond emotions. It also includes two other kinds of agility: *social agility*, which is the ability to work in complex social environments and navigate complex social relationships, and *cultural agility*, which is the capability to function effectively in a variety of cultural contexts.[48]

Negotiation and persuasion are the main skills that communicative agility brings to leadership. It enables you to hold several—perhaps conflicting—perspectives in mind simultaneously, not dismissing any but rather considering them with a sense of empathy and constructive collaboration. And, of course, there is wit and the art of swift repartee.

For instance, as the story goes, William Seward, the secretary of state in Abraham Lincoln's cabinet, came upon Lincoln at the White House, and found him polishing his shoes. The secretary gasped, "Mr. President! Sir, in Washington, we do not black our own shoes!" Lincoln replied, "Well, Mr. Secretary, whose shoes do you black?"[49] While the wit is apparent in Lincoln's repartee, the remark at the same time conveys to the secretary that he should have the sense of humility that befits public office.

Mahatma Gandhi was also famous for his wry sense of humor. In 1931, Gandhi visited London to attend a conference to discuss India's political future. A British journalist asked Gandhi what he thought of Western civilization. Gandhi famously replied, "I think it would be a good idea."

Mahatma Gandhi and the Salt March

Gandhi's Salt March of 1930 was an event that showed brilliant communicative agility. After the leaders of India's independence movement declared in December 1929 that the country should have nothing short of *purna swaraj*, or complete independence, the big question was how to achieve it.

The idea came to Gandhi like a flash in the middle of February 1930, although he did not make the idea public until early March. It suddenly struck him that mass defiance of the salt law would be an excellent communicative medium to further the goals of Indian independence.[50] The salt law referred to the steep tax on salt that the British government in India had imposed since 1835. The aim of this tax was to facilitate the import of manufactured salt from factories in Liverpool and other English cities into India. No Indian could make salt despite India's forty-six-hundred-mile peninsular coastline; Indians had to buy salt that came from England, and the price they paid for it included a tax that went to the British government in India. About 2 percent of the government's revenues came from the salt tax.[51]

Gandhi's choice to defy the salt law seemed a strange

one—there was nothing momentous about salt. The British viceroy Lord Irwin, upon learning about the salt satyagraha, wrote to London, "At present the prospect of a salt campaign does not keep me awake at night."[52] The Calcutta-based, British-owned Indian newspaper *The Statesman* scoffed: "It is difficult not to laugh, and we imagine that will be the mood of most thinking Indians. There is something almost childishly theatrical in challenging in this way the salt monopoly of the Government."[53]

> *For Gandhi, salt provided many communicative advantages.*

However, for Gandhi, salt provided many communicative advantages: First, as a universally consumed ingredient, salt cut across religious and class lines, uniting Hindus and Muslims, and rich and poor. Second, the message of a resistance to the salt tax would reach Western audiences, where public opinion about Indian independence efforts had been apathetic until then, and the immorality of levying a tax on poor people through as essential an item as common salt could generate sympathy for the movement in the First World.[54] Third, to break the salt law one could do any of a long list of prohibited actions: make salt illegally; possess, buy, or sell illegally made salt; or even encourage others to break the salt law. And this long list meant that people could participate in the movement in many ways; thus the salt satyagraha would help in generating widespread nonviolent resistance by the Indian people.

The March to Dandi

Gandhi also realized that a one-time act of breaking the salt tax law would not be very effective in creating sustained resistance to British rule. To do this, the action would have to follow a prolonged script and conclude with a climax—it had to be scripted like a drama. Thus the concept of a salt march emerged. With less than a month to his target date of March 12, Gandhi began to plan the details.

Gandhi and a few select nonviolent followers would walk 241 miles in twenty-four days to reach Dandi, a small village on the west coast of India, where they would make salt from the waters of the Arabian Sea. Millions across India would be invited to break the salt law in enactments both simultaneous and subsequent to Gandhi's actions. For instance, while thousands on various seafronts in Bombay (now Mumbai) and Karachi (now in Pakistan) would break the salt law, synchronizing with Gandhi, about twelve hundred miles to the south, Chakravarti Rajagopalachari (another famous leader) would wait for two weeks before he would lead a similar band of nonviolent volunteers to make salt in the Bay of Bengal, on the opposite side of the country.

The notion of a march also had many religious and philosophical connotations. It brought up the image of Moses leading the Israelites to the promised land, and it also echoed the difficult pilgrimages Hindus make for spiritual benefit. This metaphysical dimension added to the sense of drama and anticipation.

For a week from the time Gandhi made the announcement, on March 5, and for the twenty-four days of the march itself (from March 12 to April 6, 1930), the media and the country were abuzz with reports about the preparations for the Salt March and its progress. Updates came about how the seventy-eight (by some counts, eighty) marchers were being strictly trained to be nonviolent, about how Gandhi had decided on a band of activists who would take over if he and the others were arrested, and about how Abbas Tyabji (a Muslim) and Sarojini Naidu (a woman poet) had prominent roles in the salt satyagraha.

On March 12, Gandhi and his followers began their march, walking briskly at 6:30 a.m. from Gandhi's ashram in Ahmadabad in Gujarat. There was a sense of imminent danger, and Gandhi's speech before he set out indicated this: "Possibly these may be the last words of my life here. . . . But let there be not a semblance of breach of peace even after all of us have been arrested."[55] As they went through towns, enthusiastic crowds greeted them, hundreds of people resigned from their positions in the British government, and the hitherto circumspect Indian National Congress energetically organized similar protests across the country. The danger of repercussions—perhaps as brutal as in Jallianwala Bagh eleven years before[56]—constantly hung over the march. However, the British administration was caught in a dilemma: was the Salt March momentous enough to require them to arrest Gandhi or would they unnecessarily be making him a martyr?

While the British government in India struggled with this dilemma, Gandhi's march continued to progress and to inspire. Gandhi used the media tremendously well, exhorting reporters from India and across the world with statements like "I want world sympathy in this battle of Right against Might." With all the British dillydallying, when Gandhi finally reached Dandi, there were no British police there to arrest him or his followers. Gandhi picked up a handful of salty earth, showed it to all assembled, and, holding up this more than a pinch of salt, in his witty style remarked, "With this I shake the foundations of the British Empire!"[57] For the British, though, it was certainly not a facetious remark or gratuitous act, and certainly not for the millions of Indians. Across the country, there was an outpouring of support, tens of thousands of people broke the salt law, thousands were arrested, and many resigned from government jobs.

Gandhi did not stop there. To ensure that the message would be heard, he had drawn up a plan.

In the early hours of May 21, 1930, a group of Gandhi's followers led by Sarojini Naidu raided the British-run salt factory at Dharasana, twenty-five miles from Dandi. Naidu had been strategically chosen because she was a woman. Gandhi had announced the second march beforehand and the well-armed British were waiting for the group. Here the British made a remarkably unintelligent move—they used brute force against the nonviolent activists, hitting them with steel-tipped batons, cracking skulls and spilling blood. Webb Miller, an intrepid American journalist working with the US-based United Press International, had managed to reach remote Dharasana, walking many miles under the hot summer sun. He watched in amazement and horror as unarmed rows of volunteers moved forward to the factory's fences and without even lifting up their arms to protect themselves, allowed themselves to be felled by the policemen. Their places were taken by others in line, and as the sickening drama continued to unfold, Webb Miller started to telegraph his reports to his offices in

New York; suspecting censorship by the British, he also sent hard copies by airmail to both the London and New York offices of UPI. His reports were published and republished in more than 1,350 newspapers across the world. They were read into the US Senate records.

The result was exactly what Gandhi had planned. World sympathy was now firmly with the Indians struggling for independence; the world no longer saw the British as benevolent and caring but as ruthless, savage, and exploitative tyrants. Gandhi had won with communicative agility. After this turning point, the British began to lose control over India, and seventeen years later, after 350 years of having exploited India, the British left the country.

The Case of Rudy Giuliani

A contrasting example is that of Rudy Giuliani, the former mayor of New York City, showing how a public individual can do serious harm to his image because of faulty communicative agility.

The events of September 11, 2001, in New York City left the world shocked. People across America, and perhaps across the world, sat staring at their television screens in awe and through tears as they watched the heartbreaking destruction of buildings and human lives by the barbaric terrorist act on the World Trade Center. As the United States, with grim resolution, began its task of recovering what came to be known as Ground Zero, one figure stood out in the recovery efforts—with his megaphone and his yellow helmet, Rudy Giuliani, the mayor of New York City. Barking orders, standing in the thick of the action, leading from the front, Giuliani was the epitome of leadership.

This was in keeping with the image that Giuliani had built for himself over the years. As US attorney in the 1980s, Giuliani became nationally famous for his prosecution of high-profile cases—the junk bond trader Michael Milken, the drug mafia, and governmental corruption were all pursued and prosecuted under his direction. His most notable prosecution was that of the five mafia families, through which the back of organized crime in New York City was broken. Most defendants, like the dreaded John Gotti, boss of the Gambino family—who had earned the sobriquet Teflon Don for being "untouchable"—were sentenced to serve lifelong prison terms. Around this time, statistics began to show that crime in New York had fallen dramatically, and this drop was attributed to Giuliani's policing efforts. So it was little surprise, then, that Giuliani was seen as someone who exemplified leadership through operational agility.

Giuliani for President

The presidential campaign of 2008 saw Rudy Giuliani run as a candidate in the Republican primaries. Soon he was a front-runner, holding up in, or even leading, opinion polls that matched him against the possible Democratic candidate Hillary Clinton. But equally soon, his candidacy began to unravel—and this unraveling can be traced to his lack of agility in areas other than operational. For instance, Giuliani quickly provided a demonstration of how inept he was at communicative agility.

In an off-the-cuff remark, he claimed that he had been at the Ground Zero site "as often, if not more, than most workers." *The New York Times* soon found that his own appointment logs showed that following 9/11, Giuliani had spent only twenty-nine hours at the site in three months—as much as some workers did in three days. His subsequent assertion that his claim about his presence at Ground Zero was only to demonstrate his solidarity with workers came across as weak and defensive.

He then provided another example of poor communicative agility. While making a speech to the National Rifle Association on September 21, 2007, Giuliani, unusually for a campaigning candidate, received a call on his cell phone and answered it. It was his wife, Judith

Nathan Giuliani, he told the nonplussed audience. What the audience heard was this: "Let's see now. This is my wife calling . . . Hello, dear. I'm talking, I'm talking to the members of the NRA right now. Would you like to say hello? I love you—and I'll give you a call as soon as I'm finished. Okay? Okay, have a safe trip. Bye-bye . . . Talk to you later, dear. I love you."

The Giuliani campaign used this episode to paint a soft image of its candidate—as someone who loved his family and was caring. Maria Comella, his spokesperson, said, "What you saw today was a candidate in a spontaneous moment on the campaign trail." Unfortunately, it turned out that Giuliani had had this "spontaneous moment" a number of times previously—the *Wall Street Journal* counted forty times—and people began to see it as a gimmick. An article in the *Washington Post* called the episodes a "stunt."[58] Rudy Giuliani soon withdrew from the presidential race.

What Communicative Agility Does

Communicative agility helps people solve problems together. It creates a collaborative environment that fosters trust and confidence. As a result, people become focused on collective good rather than on individual gain. Since communicative agility relies on both verbal and nonverbal cues, it helps to convey feelings of empathy and solidarity through speech, writing, expressions, gestures, and body language.

When Should You Use Communicative Agility?

You will need to use communicative agility in any context that demands empathy or requires you to see things from another's perspective. It's also called for when you're running a meeting where people have diverse opinions and agendas, and you want to bring them into one-leadership decision. As Doris Kearns Goodwin has brilliantly documented in her book *Team of Rivals*, Abraham Lincoln's leadership, in fact, thrived on getting outstanding people who held divergent views together in his cabinet, and getting them to work together toward a common purpose—the good of the nation.[59]

Communicative agility is an absolute necessity whenever persuasion is needed—whether a single individual, a group of people, or an entire market of customers has to be persuaded. The events surrounding the *Amistad*, a ship that landed with slaves in nineteenth-century America, highlight the importance of a convincing and honest story in persuading a jury. John Quincy Adams, the former president of the United States, had only one question for the people seeking his help in representing the African men aboard the *Amistad*: "In a courtroom, whoever tells the best story wins. . . . What is their story?"

The Tylenol Story

On October 11, 1982, *Newsweek*'s cover-page article began: "Twelve-year-old Mary Kellerman of Elk Grove Village [a suburb of Chicago] awoke at dawn last Wednesday with a sore throat and a runny nose. Her parents gave her one Extra-Strength Tylenol capsule and at 7 a.m. . . . they found her dying on the bathroom floor."[60]

Within a few days, six other people had died in Chicago and other suburbs, three in one family. The cause of these seven deaths was quickly discovered when investigators traced the common thread: Tylenol Extra Strength capsules. The popular pain-relieving medicine that came in smooth gelatin-based and easy-to-swallow capsules had been poisoned.

Johnson & Johnson, the pharmaceutical company that owned Tylenol's maker, McNeil Consumer Products, first heard about Tylenol's involvement in the poisonings when its public relations department got a call from a reporter seeking a comment on the crisis. Robert

Andrews, assistant director for public relations at that time, recalled later, "In that first call we learned more from the reporter than he did from us."[61]

As word spread, there was panic across the USA. Tylenol was in virtually every home—with 37 percent of the market share, it was the bestselling over-the-counter pain and fever reliever in the US market. But, as one Chicago stockbroker said, "The name Tylenol [became] linked with poison in people's minds."[62] Chicago's police issued warnings from their cars on the streets, the FDA told customers not to use Tylenol, and the three national networks frequently carried stories on the Tylenol poisonings. The Illinois attorney general, Tyrone Fahner, claimed the most likely suspect was "a disgruntled employee in the production chain." This was not good news for Johnson & Johnson.

About 100 million people used Tylenol, which earned $300–$400 million for Johnson & Johnson every year. Tylenol sales exceeded the combined sales of the next four leading painkillers in the market—Anacin, Bayer, Bufferin, and Excedrin. In fact, during the first three quarters of 1982, Tylenol had provided 19 percent of Johnson & Johnson's corporate profits. Had Tylenol been a corporate entity unto itself, profits would have placed it in the top half of the Fortune 500.

The negative reports associated with Tylenol were

going to have a drastic effect on the company. *News-week*'s cover story reported that some state health departments had gone far beyond the FDA's warning; while the FDA warning covered Tylenol in capsule form, some state health departments banned sales of Tylenol in all forms, including tablets and liquids. In San Francisco, the public was asked not to flush Tylenol down toilets, because if the capsules contained cyanide they could poison the sewer system. The advertising guru Jerry Della Femina declared to the *New York Times* that we would not see the name Tylenol in any form within a year. Johnson & Johnson's stock price had already dipped by 3 percent in less than a week.

James Burke, CEO of Johnson & Johnson, swiftly formed a seven-member team that included a senior executive from public relations. The team had two issues before it: how should the company save people and how should the company save the product? Johnson & Johnson had quickly concluded that the problem was not in its process or with some disgruntled employee—the affected batches had been produced in factories in different cities.

One of the first things the team realized was that they needed to assure the public that this was not a Johnson & Johnson production problem. They issued a public statement about the quality-control mechanisms they had in place. Then, working with local police, they established and made public the fact that the affected stores were all in the Chicago area and nowhere else, and, further, that the batch numbers of the contaminated capsules meant that they were produced in different plants, ruling out the possibility that someone or some process in Johnson & Johnson's production had played a role in the poisoning. Illinois governor James Thompson concurred: "We have a madman out there," he declared.

Simultaneously, Johnson & Johnson announced its endorsement of the FDA warning. In what came to be seen as a remarkable act of candor, it sent 450,000 telex messages to doctors and hospitals, warning them against the use of Tylenol. And, like any company that is savvy with public relations, it stopped all advertising of Tylenol. Instead, using the media, it told consumers across the country not to use Tylenol products until matters were settled; it also announced that it was withdrawing 930,000 bottles of Tylenol capsules from the Chicago market. And then, when there were some false scares in other cities, it announced a nationwide recall of Tylenol capsules—a total of 31 million bottles at a cost of over $100 million. In all this, the public face of Tylenol was not some PR spokesperson, it was the CEO, James Burke, himself, appearing on the three networks, on various TV shows and radio programs, sympathizing with the public, taking responsibility for the company's mistakes such as not making tamperproof bottles, and explaining the company's actions, including efforts to make the medicine tamperproof going forward.

Once the suspect batches were out of the market, and people were reassured of its safety, slowly, the written-off brand of Tylenol began to pick up. Coupled with massive promotion efforts, such as providing $2.50 coupons, in a year it was back to 30 percent market share. A pharmaceutical phoenix had risen thanks to communicative agility.

In 2000, Bill Clinton awarded James Burke the Presidential Medal of Freedom. In 2003, *Fortune* magazine named him one of history's ten greatest CEOs, and thanks to his communicative skills in a dire crisis, he's remembered that way to this day.

The Ford Explorer–Firestone Tires Story

While Johnson & Johnson provides an excellent example of a company using communicative agility well, many companies suffer greatly because they don't. From the 1990s emerges a clear example in the Ford Explorer tire crisis. In the late 1990s, drivers began to find that tire treads on Ford's Explorer SUVs would peel off while the vehicle was running. The US National Highway Traffic Safety Administration (NHTSA) issued notices to both Ford and the tire manufacturer, Firestone. According to the NHTSA, hundreds of accidents and the deaths of forty-six people were related to this problem. Several independent studies showed the NHTSA figure to be very conservative—in its study, the *St. Petersburg Times* claimed forty-one people had been killed in Florida alone.[63] Later estimates suggested that 271 people had died across the country because of this design problem. The NHTSA notices were actually late on the scene—consumers had begun to sue Ford in 1991, with the first lawsuit claiming death filed in 1993.

So what did Ford and Firestone do? Instead of quickly reacting and responding to customers, the two companies began to blame each other. Hundreds of lawsuits followed, including some class action suits. Three months after the NHTSA notices, Firestone recalled 6.5 million tires, spending about $440 million on recall-related costs; Ford replaced 13 million tires on the Explorer on its own; and Ford and Firestone ended a nearly hundred-year-old partnership. Amid all this, Ford Explorer's sales declined, affecting the earnings of both companies.[64]

Shadow Traits of Communicative Agility

As we've seen with the other agilities, an overreliance on communicative agility can create problems of its own. Some of the negative traits of an overdeveloped and overused communicative agility are approval-seeking behaviors, empty talk that results in false promises, and overriding the decision-making process with melodrama.

Approval Seeking

Since communicative agility leads by building consensus and creating collaboration, if you rely too much on communicative agility, you may unconsciously develop approval-seeking habits. As a result, you would hesitate before making tough decisions that may be necessary but unpopular. Excessive communicative agility can also make you rely too much on others—subordinates and colleagues, for instance—during the decision-making process. Rather than being consultative, you become dependent, ceding your leadership to groupthink, which often results in a morass of inaction and cloudy judgment.

Empty Talk

Overdependence on communicative agility may make you lead with the mouth—with unbridled communicative agility you may unwisely make promises that can't be kept or claims that can't be justified. You will lack the check of operational agility, which determines what is practical, or the restraint of analytical agility, which weighs the pros and cons of decisions, or the far-sightedness of visionary agility, which stays focused on what is ethical and wise. You can imagine a salesperson overusing communicative agility and making implausible promises to buyers—the promises come back to bite later because they impose costs and efforts on the company far beyond the profits of the sale. If you overuse communicative agility, you may win the sales battles, but you will lose the long-term war of consistently strong performance over time.

Melodrama

Well-developed communicative agility enables you to become sensitive, both to the needs of others and to the needs of the situation. With communicative agility, you also become aware of how words and actions can persuade or dissuade others. With overactive communicative agility, however, you can end up doing too much "reading between the lines." It begins to look as if things are not what they seem to be: there are hidden agendas and cabals, and coups in the making—conspiracy theories abound. In short, when communicative agility is in hyperdrive, ordinary events will have as much melodrama as a daytime soap opera. Such hypersensitive reading of people and situations leads to emotion-dominated behaviors, and hasty and drastic action.

How Too Much
Communicative Agility Can Destroy

In 2007, a young graduate student in public policy at the University of Chicago dropped out of the master's program—Andrew Mason had been tempted by the offer Eric Lefkofsky, a venture capitalist, had made to invest a million dollars in Mason's start-up idea. The start-up, a website called ThePoint.org, focused on online fundraising. It built on the realization that if people could see others contributing to the same cause as they were, they would contribute more or feel their contributions made more of a difference. Mason also introduced another condition, which gave the site its name. By this condition—

called the "tipping point"—contributors' credit cards would not be charged unless a prespecified goal was met for each fundraising effort, and this made it less risky for donors by ensuring that they would not be contributing to a project that would fail for lack of funds. It was a great idea, and still drives many online crowdfunding companies, like Kickstarter. After a year, however, the site was going nowhere, and Eric Lefkofsky was getting impatient at the lack of progress. Mason reworked the business model based on what he had learned in the business so far.

In an interview with the *Wall Street Journal*, he revealed his lessons. First, he had discovered that Internet-based companies that push altruistic interests do not succeed. So, ThePoint.org would have to be refashioned to cater to selfish interests. The second lesson Mason had learned was that you can't work with an abstract idea.[65] The tipping point needed a focus. And so emerged a new company, Groupon. Its idea was simple: the site would focus on promoting local businesses—it would offer coupons to customers for at least one deal from a local business in their city every day. But again, as in ThePoint .org, the tipping point condition would kick in—the deal would become activated (or "tip") only if a certain prespecified number of customers bought the coupon from Groupon; if not, the credit cards of people who had signed up would not be charged. Thus the name

Groupon ("group" plus "coupon"). Groupon would charge customers once a deal had tipped and would pay the local business 50 percent of the revenues.

The model paid off for two reasons: First, unlike Facebook or Twitter, which offered free services, Groupon made money off every customer who bought a coupon. Second, it played the "network effects" model (see chapter 4) tremendously well in two ways—people who liked it and signed up for a deal would encourage their friends to sign up as well so they could get the numbers to tip the deal, and, further, the Groupon site (or e-mail service) itself became rapidly popular because of the network effect created by people telling each other about it.

Groupon also capitalized on the value that customers place on relatively scarce goods. Marketing psychologist Robert Cialdini calls it the "scarcity principle": "Sometimes all that is necessary to make people want something more is to tell them that before long they can't have it."[66] Jonah Berger has pointed out, in his recent book *Contagious*, that not only does scarcity increase demand but if a product or service is available in limited quantities, customers want to tell (brag to) others about how they got it, and thus create a network effect.[67]

After the first test deal, for a local pizza shop, in October 2008—a "buy one get one free" offer—Groupon launched officially in November 2008. Within sixteen months, its valuation was touching $1 billion—the fastest company to do that after YouTube, which did it in twelve months—and it had more than 350 employees. As the number of deals offered every day increased, revenues exploded.

In November 2009, one year after it began, Groupon on average offered seventeen deals every day (an 82 percent increase from November 2008), and by April 2010, Groupon offered thirty-one coupons on average every day (a whopping 250 percent increase from its first month in business). The revenues were similarly going through the sky—fourteen thousand dollars every day one year later, and more than forty thousand per day eighteen months later. Groupon's gross income grew by an eye-popping 2,500 percent in its second year. The *Wall Street Journal* compared this to second-year growth rates of other dot-com companies: Google (2004): 352 percent; Amazon (1997): 838 percent; Salesforce.com (2003): 128 percent; and eBay (1998): 724 percent.[68]

This is where communicative agility comes into the picture. While Internet companies in Silicon Valley employed computer geeks skilled in programming languages, Groupon sought employees who had a way with words—they were employed as marketing copywriters who wrote enticing text to attract coupon buyers or as savvy salespeople who built relationships with select local businesses. Chicago has often been ranked America's funniest city, with its famous improv-comedy industry; Groupon found there a ready supply of young witty people for its marketing and sales positions.

The *Wall Street Journal* provided the example of an ad for a skydiving deal: "Skydiving is the perfect way to celebrate a birthday, sweat out premarital terror for a bachelor or bachelorette party, or take a glorious leap into a new life as a migratory swallow." The *New York Times* attributed Groupon's success with words to the fact that it "mixed tools and terms from journalism, softened the traditional heavy hand of advertising, added some banter and attitude and married the result to a discounted deal." The paper described how one of Groupon's ad campaigns—for a one-hour horse ride at half price at a stable in Michigan—ended in more than 270 people buying the limited-time offer. Sure enough, there was exponential growth in Groupon's subscriber base.

Soon Google came courting. It offered to buy Groupon for a whopping $6 billion, an offer that Groupon audaciously turned down with an eye on its own initial public offering (IPO). As it cruised to its IPO, venture capitalists rushed in with another $950 million in investment. It was now catering to 375 cities and thirty-five countries, and adding almost a dozen cities a week. It made its IPO on November 4, 2011, on the NASDAQ exchange, raising

$700 million (second only to Google's $1.7 billion offering in 2004). Groupon was valued at $12.8 billion, more than two times what Google had offered.

But Communicative Agility Alone Is Not Enough

By November 12, 2012, just after the first anniversary of the IPO, the company narrative was very different. It was becoming apparent that the Groupon story was turning out to be as unrealistic as any fairy tale. Its $20 share was selling at $2.69, nearly 90 percent below its opening price. For all its wit, Groupon was clearly a laughingstock, a failed stand-up routine. Andrew Mason was fired as CEO in February 2013. But Groupon never really recovered. Its stock price has hovered around $4 since September 2015.

What happened? We get a hint from Mason's final letter to Groupon employees, in which he says, in his wickedly funny way, "After four and a half intense and wonderful years as CEO of Groupon, I've decided that I'd like to spend more time with my family. Just kidding—I was fired today. If you're wondering why . . . you haven't been paying attention."

What happened was that Groupon had prioritized

communicative agility at the expense of the other agilities—and was paying the price for it. Let me explain how it lacked other agilities.

Analytical Agility on the Back Burner

Groupon did not seem to exercise analytical agility; in fact, it became questionable whether Groupon possessed enough of it at all.

As Groupon was preparing its IPO, the company used an unconventional financial metric, which it called adjusted consolidated segment operating income (ACSOI). ACSOI was income calculated after excluding marketing costs, which made up the bulk of the company's expenses. As a result, ACSOI made Groupon's financial results appear better than they actually were. After the Securities and Exchange Commission (SEC) raised questions about the metric—which the *Wall Street Journal* called "financial voodoo"—Groupon downplayed ACSOI in its IPO documents.

Groupon's sales teams—well equipped verbally but not analytically—drew up campaigns for local merchants that hurt them financially. Merchants collaborating with Groupon had to offer discounts of at least 50 percent and were led to set abnormally high limits in terms of the number of customers for whom the offer would hold or in terms of the time periods for which the offer would be valid. As a result, small merchants would be flooded with large numbers of low-paying customers, sometimes for long periods.

The *New York Times* was soon writing a different kind of story about Groupon: it recounted the tales of merchants who were complaining about having to take loans to meet the operating expenses to serve these customers. In a leaked internal memo that the *Wall Street Journal* published, Eric Lefkofsky, who had taken over as CEO, wrote to Groupon employees, "Yet we all know our operational and financial performance has eroded the confidence of many of our supporters, both inside and outside of the company."

Lack of Inventive Agility

Other commentators remarked on the fact that Groupon did not have any specialty in its offering that would prevent others from copying its business model. Indeed, by the time of its IPO more than five hundred companies across the world were imitating Groupon, from the Amazon-funded Groupon duplicate LivingSocial to niche players like BlackBizScope, which catered to

African Americans. In such circumstances, where there are low barriers to entry, sustainability of the business becomes possible only through repeated innovation. You have to keep competitors playing catch-up. And, unfortunately, Groupon showed no such inventive agility.

Lack of Visionary Agility

Underlying Groupon's fall was a tremendous lack of visionary agility—an incredible sense of carpe diem dominated the spirit of the company that focused singularly on the short term. There was no conceptualization of growth over the long haul. Any question that dealt with either of the visionary elements—what is the long-term impact or how widespread will this impact be?—became taboo in the soda-water environment created around the free-flowing words and the gaseous venture-capitalist funds available to Groupon. Questions such as "What would make customers come back to the merchants who were offering coupons?" or "What would make merchants come back to Groupon again and again?" never came up for the management team. Ultimately, with its exclusive focus on communicative agility, Groupon itself turned out to be just another fast-talking flash sale unable to sustain itself over time.

Chapter 7

//

Visionary Agility: Going Beyond the Here and Now

R ICHARD ATTENBOROUGH'S IMMENSELY successful three-hour-long epic movie *Gandhi* was released in 1982, unusually hitting screens in India a week before audiences in America and England got to see it. I was one of the thousands of enthusiastic young college students in Bangalore who thronged the theaters and saw the movie within the first week of its release. Jack Kroll reviewed it in *Newsweek*: "Attenborough mounts a powerful challenge to his audience by presenting Gandhi as the most profound and effective of revolutionaries, creating out of a fierce personal discipline a chain reaction that led to tremendous historical consequences. At a time of deep political unrest, economic dislocation, and nuclear anxiety, seeing *Gandhi* is an experience that will change many minds and hearts."[69] I was one of those profoundly affected. Thirty-five years later, as I sit down to write this chapter, a particularly vivid scene displaying Gandhi's visionary agility immediately surfaces in my mind.

Let me give you the context for that scene. In August 1947, in the wake of the partition of India, Calcutta was ravaged with rampaging mobs of both Hindus and Muslims looting and killing. Police had been called in but had failed to stop the rioting and violence. The army too had proved ineffectual. Gandhi reached Calcutta and declared that he would not eat or drink until the violence abated. A friend tried to talk him out of it, but Gandhi replied that the fast had to be now or never. It would be too late afterward. He was firm: "The minority Muslims cannot be left in a perilous state. My fast has to be preventive if it is to be any good." A calculation he had made was that if his tactic worked in Calcutta, he would be able to handle the violence and communal killing in Punjab, on the border on the other side of India, too. At the same time, he was able to envisage and articulate the negative fallout of his failure: "If I falter now, the conflagration may spread, and soon, I can see clearly, two or three powers will be upon us and thus will end our short-lived dream of independence."[70]

For several days, in spite of Gandhi's fast, the rioting continued—all of Calcutta was on fire as the rioting mobs continued to kill each other. Finally, as Gandhi became increasingly weak, and leaders from both Hindu and Muslim communities appealed for peace, the violence began to subside.

The scene in Attenborough's *Gandhi* begins with a bunch of tough-looking Hindu men laying down their weapons—rusty knives and swords and country guns—at Gandhi's feet. He seems very weak and continues to lie in a cot, watching them. They tell him, "These are Hindu arms; we promise we will not fight anymore." Gandhi blesses them in a faint voice, "Go—God be with you."

The men stand for a moment, as if in reverence, and then turn to leave. Suddenly, a wild-eyed man rushes through the throng of departing men and moves violently toward Gandhi. He throws a chapati on Gandhi's chest and says forcefully, "Eat!" He takes a step toward Gandhi and again tells him, "Eat! I do not want to go to hell with your death on my soul." His face is contorted with wild emotion—a volatile mixture of anger, sadness, and bitterness.

Gandhi replies calmly, "Only God decides who goes to hell." The man stares down angrily at Gandhi for a long moment—it is obvious that he is under tremendous stress; he has no words, but when speech comes after the pause, it bursts out as a confession: "I killed a child . . . I smashed his head against the wall!"

Gandhi winces, taken aback by the horror of the act; he barely manages a response: "Why?"

"They killed my son! The Muslims killed my son!" the man replies, holding his hand hip high to indicate the boy's height.

There is a long moment of silence as the words hang in the air; all that can be heard is the sound of the man's rasping sobs as he is overcome with emotion. One senses that he is filled with remorse and is struggling to come to terms with his reprehensible act.

Then Gandhi says, "I know a way out of hell."

His voice is quite firm, and the note of confidence makes the man look up from his sobbing with some hope.

"Find a child—a child whose mother and father have been killed. A little boy—about this high." Gandhi holds his hand at the same height as the man had.

"Raise him as your own. Only, be sure that he is a Muslim. And that you raise him as one."

The man stiffens because it is a tough task, but it is also a visionary solution, offering a path for penance and reconciliation. He turns to leave and takes a step toward the door. But suddenly he veers around and, weeping, bends to clutch Gandhi's feet and rests his forehead on them. Gandhi reaches out and touching the top of his head whispers, "God bless you . . . Go."

This episode from Gandhi's life is a classic illustration of visionary agility. An unanticipated situation presents itself—a man who killed a child as retribution for his own child's murder is suffering with guilt and perhaps unacknowledged remorse for what he has done. His unexpected confession is as much a cry for help to Gandhi. As the script for the movie makes plain, beneath all his bluster and bravado the man is tender, hurting.[71] Gandhi, despite his physical weakness, is quick to recognize this. His visionary agility is initially challenged by the horrific revelation, enhanced by the medieval barbarism of the act, and an involuntary "Why?" escapes his lips. But he recovers quickly to offer a solution—the radical solution lies in adopting a Muslim boy and bringing him up as a Muslim.

That solution, more than any legal sentence or any moral upbraiding, offers both punishment and hope. The punishment is that the adopted child will remind the man every day of his own barbarous act, but at the same time, the hope is that the child will offer a way forward and a promise for the future. Also, there is hope that by raising a Muslim child the man will understand more of Islam, which, as a result, will foster communal harmony. The solution goes beyond the resolution of the man's grief, remorse, and learning. It extends to society, where a Muslim child—any child—orphaned during the riots may find a new home, new family, and parents who have lost their children, like this man, may find solace by adopting a child.

Visionary Agility: Seeing Far, Seeing Wide

Among the five agilities, visionary is the most important. When you use visionary agility, you take a long-term and an expansive view of the world. The long-term view gives you the ability to anticipate future impacts of current decisions and actions, while the expansive view makes you aware of the interests and predicaments of others beyond yourself or your organization. While all the other four agilities are necessary, only visionary agility provides the strategic perspective. Thus, in order for any individual's or organization's leadership decision or action to go beyond the short term, it is absolutely necessary that it be evaluated through the lens of visionary agility.

Only visionary agility provides the strategic perspective.

When Visionary Agility Goes MIA

The Green Revolution in India

In the 1960s the world was going through a hunger crisis. Many countries didn't have enough food for their rapidly growing populations. Agricultural scientists across the world were trying hard to improve crop yields and agricultural production. Norman Borlaug, an American scientist working in Mexico, arrived at a set of agricultural practices that boosted wheat yields manifold. This set of practices came to be called the Green Revolution.

At this time, India was no exception to the hunger crisis, and its self-sufficiency in terms of food was being severely challenged. It was reeling under an explosion in population with no increase in agricultural production. The Indian government's massive efforts to promote celibacy and the use of contraceptives had failed, agricultural production that depended heavily on the erratic monsoon could not produce the food necessary for this vast population, and predictions of terrible famines abounded. In such a scenario, the productive methods of the new Green Revolution offered much promise.

The Indian government chose the northwestern state of Punjab for a Green Revolution experiment. Scientists studied the Punjab farmer's agricultural habits and concluded that he was farming very inefficiently. First, he depended too much on open irrigation sources like lakes and rivers, which were very vulnerable to the vagaries of nature. Second, the Punjab farmer did not use any chemical fertilizers or pesticides, even when scientific studies had shown that agricultural productivity improved dramatically if one did. Third, the Punjab farmer grew crops for only half the year; he left his fields fallow for the other half.

Proponents of the Green Revolution, with immense support from the Indian government, suggested several remedies. They brought in hybrid wheat and rice seeds from the United States, they introduced fertilizers and pesticides into the Punjab farming practice, they promoted yearlong farming, and, most important, they began to tap groundwater through bore wells that were sunk across the land. Further, the Indian government guaranteed the farmer a minimum price for his grain, subsidized the well and equipment to pump groundwater, and provided free electricity to power the pump.

All this paid off—at least in the short term. Within two decades, rice yields improved dramatically from a dismal two tons per hectare (roughly 2.5 acres) to an astounding six tons per hectare. After adjusting for inflation and exchange rates, the price of rice dropped from approximately \$550 (fifteen thousand rupees) a ton in the 1970s to \$200 (seven thousand rupees) a ton in the 1990s.[72]

But the story doesn't end there. The predicament of the Punjab farmer today calls the success of the Green Revolution strongly into question—and the problems can be directly traced to a lack of visionary agility. Despite the good intentions of the promoters of the Green Revolution, its techniques have led to many detrimental effects that could have been avoided had more visionary agility been exercised. For example, the officials promoted rampant use of fertilizers and pesticides. Not only did this spur the growth of pests resistant to chemicals, but it also severely depleted the fertility of the soil. A forward-looking approach would have warned the illiterate farmer of the negative consequences of excessively chemical-based agriculture. A simple oversight, for instance, was in the Hindi word used for "pesticide": *dava*, which translates as "medicine." And medicine, of course, is more associated with curing than with the chemical harshness associated with pesticides. As a result, farmers liberally used fertilizers and pesticides.

In addition, the practice of planting twice a year further took a toll on the land, leading to loss of fertility. Although it is now discouraged by the government, and has in fact been declared illegal in some places, the practice persists. Many farmers are just too tempted by what they've seen in previous years.

But the biggest problem is that farmers are not able to find groundwater—inadequate planning led to a significant fall in groundwater levels. Farmers who used to be able to get water fifty feet below the surface must now pump water from three hundred, five hundred, and sometimes one thousand feet.

Deeper wells demand more powerful, and more expensive, pump sets, which the average farmer cannot afford despite the farms' being more profitable than before. He therefore borrows money from local moneylenders because banks and official sources of loans are not forthcoming. The debt situation that has eternally plagued the Indian farmer has started all over again for the Punjab farmer. Many farmers have committed suicide by consuming the very pesticide that was supposed to improve crop productivity.[73]

Visionary agility would have enabled consideration of the long-term impact of the Green Revolution on groundwater, and perhaps tempered its use; additionally, groundwater replenishment methods, such as rainwater harvesting, would have been conceived and promoted. All things considered, the Green Revolution in India provides a classic illustration of how good efforts, despite the best of intentions and headiness of initial success, can have a dismal and dire impact in the long term if visionary agility does not play its role of considering the long-term implications and the breadth of impact of the decision you are making today.

The Green Revolution example also tells us about something very significant: visionary agility is not only about ethics. Of course it makes you think beyond yourself, to think about others, but perhaps more important, visionary agility enables you to think beyond the now, to envision the future as you make decisions today.

> *Visionary agility enables you to think beyond the now.*

What Visionary Agility Does

Long-Term Lens

With visionary agility, even though you know you're in a dynamic, unpredictable world, you consider the various ways in which the world may unfold in the future. A consideration of these different possibilities helps you understand the strategic component of your current actions and decisions. As the story of the Green Revolution in India illustrates, projects that lack visionary agility—even if undertaken with good intentions—can result in situations that are as bad as, if not worse than, they were before.

Wide-Angle Lens: A Beyond-Me, Beyond-Company Vision

Visionary agility makes an aspiring leader adopt a worldview that is much more expansive than one that is focused on just earnings and revenues. Such a perspective allows you to examine the implications of your actions for people and processes that are beyond the realm of immediate results.

Jim Stengel, ex–global marketing officer of Procter & Gamble, found that the world's top fifty companies, which on average grow three times faster than their competitors (and in some cases ten times faster), all have at their core one common principle: "focus on fundamental human values that improve people's lives."[74]

You don't need to be a rocket scientist or a selfless saint to get the lesson: thinking beyond your own narrow interest has economic benefits. What visionary agility tells you is *how to do it*. There are many examples of CEOs and companies that use visionary agility to see the world beyond and take actions that benefit many people and many companies. But paying attention to your visionary agility makes this become a conscious personal habit rather than an ad hoc principle.

In the opening chapters, I talked about the Indian sugar company EID Parry, which bought poor-quality sugarcane uprooted in a storm and paid its farmers the standard rates it would have paid for good quality cane. It suffered a huge financial loss, but its concern was for its farmers. We also saw how EID Parry is one of the most successful companies in its industry. We read about Roy Vagelos, the CEO of Merck, who gave away a critical medicine for free.

And then there are people like Aaron Feuerstein, the CEO of Malden Mills in Lawrence, Massachusetts. As he stood in the parking lot watching his cloth factory burn down, he announced that none of his three thousand employees would be fired. Using his insurance money, he rebuilt the factory and paid all three thousand idle workers their full salaries during the reconstruction. Six years later, the company filed for bankruptcy, and he was removed as CEO. But he said in an interview, "Maybe on paper our company is worthless to Wall Street, but I can tell you it's worth more."

Still, visionary agility does not mean that you have to be altruistic. It means that if you consider the ways your decision or action will also affect people and processes that are not directly impacted, you will make decisions that are wise and profitable for everyone.

As we'll see in the case of Burt's Bees, the company's vision becomes threefold, encompassing the company, the customers, and, in its most expansive version, the planet itself. Thus visionary agility enables us to talk about universal ethics, which go beyond religious doctrines or cultural beliefs.

Transformation of the Reactive into the Strategic

By bringing in the long-term perspective, by widening the scope of our imagination beyond the immediate, and by aspiring for the higher ideals of humanism, visionary agility transforms agility from being merely a reactive response to a change in the environment or context into a strategic capability that serves both the decision maker and many others in the long run.

When Should You Use Visionary Agility?

As is clear from the discussion so far, whenever strategic considerations are in play, visionary agility becomes mandatory. In fact, for any company or person to become a true leader, it is essential that visionary agility is being exercised constantly. If you examine your decisions and actions through the lens of visionary agility, you will make them strategically viable and long lasting.

Visionary agility helps us keep in mind larger goals and humanistic purposes amid the turmoil of everyday life and the continual adjustments we must make. Amid the turbulence of change, visionary agility keeps the focus on your values and your company's. Like the ability of the ancient mariners to follow the polestar as they navigated unknown seas, visionary agility helps you remain connected to your values as you navigate the ebb and flow of life.

Burt's Bees: The Greater Good Model

In 1984, Roxanne Quimby, a thirty-three-year-old single mother, was hitchhiking in Maine and given a ride by a beekeeper, Burt Shavitz. Shavitz was in his late forties and sported a big shaggy beard; he used to sell honey in the local markets. They fell in love, and Quimby began living with Shavitz, who led a simple life in the country with his dogs—in fact, his home was a converted turkey coop. Quimby began to make candles with the wax from Shavitz's beehives, and they sold these candles in the local markets and fairs along with Shavitz's jars of honey.

The candles began to attract customers because of their attention to detail and artistic form. In 1989, Quimby and

Shavitz got a lucky break when an upscale boutique in New York City ordered hundreds of their candles. The couple quickly hired forty workers and opened up a production facility in an abandoned bowling alley. Quimby began to experiment, using old farmers' formulas she discovered here and there, and in 1991 she started making a lip balm out of beeswax and sweet almond oil, which became a bestseller and continues to be the company's iconic and bestselling product to date. Yes, company. In 1991 they incorporated Burt's Bees—Quimby owned two-thirds of the company and Shavitz one-third. Somewhere along the way, Shavitz's shaggy beard had inspired the company logo, which appeared on all the labels and product packaging. At this point, they were selling about half a million candles a year. From the time of its founding, Burt's Bees has had "natural" at its core—in fact, the company claims that its founding belief was "Natural products work *with* your body for the best results," and that the company has never wavered from that belief.

In 1993, as the company expanded both in product lines and in revenues, Roxanne Quimby decided to move it to North Carolina, despite Burt Shavitz's reluctance to shift from Maine. Around this time, the company decided to focus only on personal care products, shelving products like the candles with which it had started. Gradually, toothpastes, shampoos, and a popular baby products line replaced the candles. The by-now incredibly profitable company invested some of its funds to buy up 185,000 acres of endangered forestland in Maine. In 2003, 80 percent of Burt's Bees was sold to AEA Investors for $141.6 million; Quimby still held 20 percent of the company.

Under a new CEO appointed by AEA, Burt's Bees began to expand further, until, in 2008, it was bought by Clorox for nearly $1 billion. Quimby got about $183 million for her stake. What is important to note is that Burt's Bees never forgot its founders' green motivations. Even as Burt's Bees started growing into a large company, the founders remained committed to their principles. As they started opening Burt's Bees stores in countries from Taiwan to Australia, they learned to cope with the expectations of large buyers like Walmart and Target and also the demands of the environmentally conscious end-customer—they learned to focus on capability building. But the company was always mindful of the message the brand communicated. For instance, on the first floor of the company's headquarters in Durham, North Carolina, they had dedicated spaces where designers would build replicas of Burt's Bees stores in other countries—whether it was an independent store in Taiwan or a kiosk in the cosmetics section of an Australian department store like David Jones or a Burt's Bees shelf in Whole Foods in America. The designers had to ensure that the various store layouts were absolutely consistent in communicating the Burt's Bees brand values and the company's commitment to environmental protection.

Taking this further, Burt's Bees has evolved a business model that it calls the Greater Good. In this model, customers, community, and the environment are as important as the company's bottom line. Burt's Bees made it a part of its organizational culture by requiring every employee to participate in at least eight hours of "value-driven" work every year: two hours doing something to improve their wellness, two hours on something that resulted in bettering the environment, and two hours doing outreach work in the community—for instance, volunteering with an organization like Habitat for Humanity. While this was easy to implement for salaried employees, it became challenging to convince part-time workers to create the space to achieve the eight hours of value-generated work. Burt's Bees thus came up with various opportunities to help the part-time workers meet this goal.

Burt's Bees provides several illustrations of visionary agility in action. Here's an example. In 2008, after being acquired by Clorox, a perceived "enemy of the environment," the company was faced with increasing attrition as employees left, perhaps suspecting that the company had betrayed its values. Burt's Bees began to invest in programs that promoted and disseminated its organizational culture and values. A culture survey was designed to answer the question, "How well do our employees know our culture and values?" An interesting relationship emerged between employee retention and the efforts to communicate the organizational culture among employees. In the years when the score from the culture survey was high (that is, employees knew more about the culture and values of Burt's Bees), attrition was lower. And in the years when the culture survey score came down, the turnover was high.[75] Thus the more aware and involved the employees were with the company's culture, the less likely they were to leave.

How are the cultural values disseminated through the company? This is done in several ways. The Greater Good business model and its eight-hour commitment is one way. And as the *New York Times* reported, there is also a strong message about concern for the environment: "Employees' bonuses are based in part on how well the company meets energy conservation goals, and there are prime parking spaces for staff members who drive hybrid cars or carpool. [The company] buys offsets for 100 percent of its carbon emissions and is working toward a goal of sending no trash to landfills by 2020."[76] From the perspective of its customers, there continues to be a tremendous emphasis on "natural," and the proportion of natural ingredients in its products has increased to an incredible 99 percent.

When Clorox acquired Burt's Bees, there was an out-
cry from many "pro-natural" customers and organizations that Burt's Bees had sold out for corporate greed.
However, Clorox loved the Burt's Bees brand and the
values it communicated. In fact, after the acquisition, a
senior executive from Clorox told the Burt's Bees team,
"It's like bringing a new baby into the household. You
have to be watchful that the brothers and sisters already
in the family don't smother the baby with their love. We
will be careful that existing divisions in the Clorox enterprise don't kill you with their love—we will keep you
at arm's distance."[77]

And true enough, in a tail-wags-the-dog story, the
hundred-year-old Clorox, which used to be on Green-
peace's attack list, is now a leader in sustainability with
its natural-ingredients-based Green Works cleaning
products, Brita water purifiers, and, of course, Burt's
Bees personal care products, which, with double-digit
growth rates, have been spearheading the healthy growth
of Clorox's lifestyle category.[78]

Shadow Traits of Visionary Agility

You might think that one can never have too much of
visionary agility. After all, what's the harm in thinking

about the long term and also being concerned about whom you're going to affect and how? Well, it's not that simple. An overactive visionary agility can create as many problems as it aims to solve.

Complacency

When you rely too much on visionary agility, to the exclusion of the other four agilities, time seems to stretch forever ahead of you. There is no urgency to do anything, because life is long. A sense of complacency sets in. An overactive visionary agility tells you that since we are in the game for the long haul, there will always be time to do what you ultimately want to achieve. As a result, there is a strong tendency to kick the can down the road—to postpone decisions and actions ad infinitum.

Not Being Rooted in the Present

If you rely too much on visionary agility, you focus so much on the big picture down the road that current details fall out of the scope of your vision. Even if you notice the smaller practical problems that are blocking your progress, your strong visionary agility makes you believe that things will work themselves out in the long run, so you don't need to respond to things that are unraveling on the ground right now. To turn a common cliché on its head: you can't see the trees for the forest.

Ignoring Reality

Because visionary agility leads you to imagine the future, if you exercise it too much and don't let the other agilities inform you, then you will tend to ignore reality and live in an imagined utopia of tomorrow. Thus when disasters hit that could have been prevented had warnings been heeded earlier, you are caught by surprise and often look outward to place blame. Carly Fiorina, the former CEO of Hewlett-Packard, and her troubled times at the company illustrate this tendency of a visionary agility that spins out of control.

Carly Fiorina and Hewlett-Packard

In July 1999, when Carly Fiorina was named CEO of Hewlett-Packard (HP), she became the first woman to head a Fortune Top 20 company. She came to HP when it was going through a crisis, and she started to remedy it immediately. She decided that HP should be the technology behemoth of the world, offering not only its profitable printer products, but everything else as well, from digital cameras to supercomputers. Fighting stiff opposition from its board of directors, including Walter Hewlett, the son of Bill Hewlett, cofounder of HP, and internal constituencies, Fiorina spearheaded HP's purchase of Compaq, the PC manufacturer.

Fiorina's excessive reliance on visionary agility, however, created a blind spot about practical on-the-ground realities: the two companies had vastly different corporate cultures, and the management found day-to-day decision making and execution difficult. According to her vision, merging two of the largest companies in the industry to create one superplayer made tremendous sense, but in the first week after the merger was announced HP's share price fell by 22 percent. "I told the boards the market would hate this deal initially," she later said. "To be honest, the reaction was a bit more negative than we thought."[79]

Soon the $80 billion HP was locked in unsuccessful battles with other PC makers—IBM, Dell, and Sony, among others. In enterprise computing, HP began to offer a middleware architecture called Adaptive Enterprise, which never took off, and consequently HP's enterprise-computing division struggled. In storage, HP lost to EMC, and in servers to Dell and IBM. Despite her decisive approach to matters and her skills as a communicator, Fiorina lost many executives, who either resigned or were fired. But, most important, due to her characteristic misplaced visionary agility, she vehemently resisted making changes at the company level in response to evolving situations, even as she made dramatic changes in the company's vision.

It is not clear whether Fiorina had anticipated what would happen on February 8, 2005: even without Walter Hewlett, who had been elbowed out by Fiorina, Hewlett-Packard's board of directors fired her. And the board's statement may offer some insight into Fiorina's lopsided approach, which favored visionary agility over others, especially operational agility. Patricia Dunn, the non-executive chairman, said, "She had a strategic vision and put in place a plan that has given HP the capabilities to compete and win. We thank Carly for her significant leadership over the past six years as we look forward to accelerating the execution of the company's strategy. . . . This is not a change related to strategy. This is a change based on a desire to accelerate that strategy. We think that requires hands-on execution."

Clearly, the board felt that Fiorina lacked operational agility. And as you will remember, in the early years of the millennium, after the dot-com bust, technology companies needed to be nimble in operations. Fiorina not only was considered inept in operational issues, but she also couldn't put together a team that could handle the nitty-gritty of operations. Fiorina's focus on big vision and strategic deal making at the expense of everyday operations ultimately led to her ouster and to HP's disappointing performance.

Agilities Table

Agility	What It Does	Where It Shines	Shadow Traits
ANALYTICAL	▪ Creates awareness: helps in understanding the "real" problem ▪ Enables objective analysis through clear logic and reasoning ▪ Continually creates, uses, and modifies a history of problem solving ▪ Transforms experience into knowledge	▪ Application of logic ▪ Sorting out ill-defined problems ▪ Objective, unbiased judgment	▪ Black-and-white thinking, inability to handle ambiguity ▪ Analysis paralysis (too absorbed in "what if?" analysis) ▪ Defensiveness (argumentative and critical of others who question the analysis)

Agility	What It Does	Where It Shines	Shadow Traits
OPERATIONAL	■ Leads through action ■ Bridges knowing and doing ■ Transforms ideas into reality	■ Agility through action ■ Leadership by example ■ Decisive action, especially in starting new projects or ending existing projects	■ Micromanagement ■ Undirected action for action's sake ■ Intimidation ■ Uncontrolled desire for action leads to win-or-lose attitudes and insensitive styles of working
Agility	What It Does	Where It Shines	Shadow Traits
INVENTIVE	■ Discerns uniqueness of individual phenomena but also perceives how they are interrelated ■ Combines seemingly unrelated phenomena in creatively productive ways ■ Transforms sensory experience into deep insight	■ Creative solutions ■ Problem solving amid ambiguity ■ Systemic, wide perspectives	■ Scattered thinking (lack of focus and inattention to detail) ■ Overcommitment (everything looks attractive, can't say no) ■ Sky-based dreaming (feet not on ground, unrealistic thinking)

Agility	What It Does	Where It Shines	Shadow Traits
COMMUNICATIVE	▪ Solves problems through mediation and participative solutions ▪ Creates an atmosphere of trust and confidence ▪ Transforms empathy into words and expressions	▪ Empathy ▪ A bringing together of diverse agendas ▪ Leadership through persuasion	▪ Oversensitivity (too much "reading between the lines") ▪ Dependence (tendency to rely on others for work, approval-seeking behaviors) ▪ Empty talk (promises that can't be kept)

Agility	What It Does	Where It Shines	Shadow Traits
VISIONARY	▪ Provides a long-term, wide-angle lens ▪ Sustains a beyond-me, beyond-company vision ▪ Transforms the reactive into the strategic	▪ Strategic vision ▪ Ethical consideration ▪ Gatekeeper in all contexts	▪ Complacency, postponed action ▪ Ignore details in search of the big picture ▪ Self-delusion (too absorbed in being visionary, not responsive to feedback) ▪ Victim mentality (when detrails happen, feel shock and blame the world)

Chapter 8

//

Working with the Five Agilities

S O FAR, I've shown you how individuals and companies have used the five agilities to become leaders and dynamic entities. But how can you apply this framework in practice so *you* can become an agile leader and make your company as nimble—and successful—as possible? In this chapter I am going to show you a structured approach to do this using the Vivékin Intelligences Framework (VIF).

My approach here has been somewhat influenced by the singular concept of the OODA loop that was conceptualized by John Boyd, one of the best American military strategists. According to Boyd, during a dogfight between two fighter pilots, each pilot goes through a loop that comprises four steps: observation, orientation, decision, and action (OODA). And the pilot who executes the OODA loop faster is the one who wins (see Figure 1).

FIGURE 1. John Boyd's OODA Loop

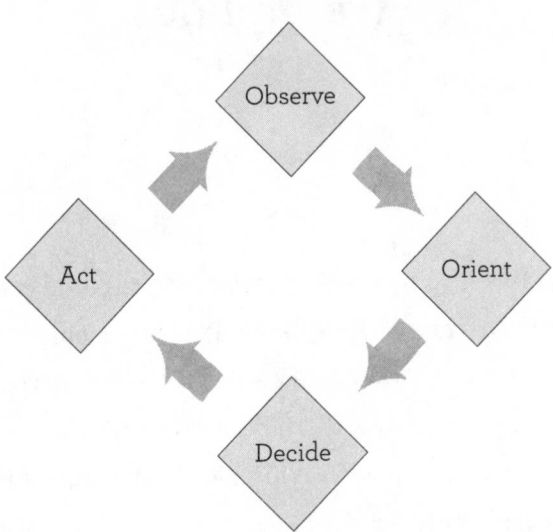

But for Boyd, the OODA loop spills over into our everyday lives because, he believed, "uncertainty is a fundamental and irresolvable characteristic of our lives, no matter how good our observations and theories for explanation are."[80] In a presentation called "Conceptual Spiral," Boyd extended the OODA loop to various organizational contexts focusing on four themes:

- uncertainty is pervasive and the prime characteristic of life
- it is essential to combine analysis with synthesis, induction with deduction
- novelty, mismatches, and creativity are critically important
- adequate orientation patterns can only emerge if we develop and combine multiple perspectives on a situation or problem

You can see how relevant Boyd's ideas are to leadership and strategy in the fast-moving, dynamically changing business environments that we have been discussing in this book. From your own experience, you know that being quick to market, having the best product, investing in innovation, and that kind of thing are essential for business success. But you also know that's not enough. What you need to do, really, is to beat your competitor—using both unpredictability and speed. You win because the other guy didn't think you'd make *that* move and move *that* fast. Agility is the key to victory. And now, after reading this far, you're in on the secret. There are five agilities, and you're adept at pulling out the right ones for the situation and mixing them up in the right ways, throwing in visionary agility so that you are also strategic.

I've told you Boyd was brilliant. He better be, because he was hands-down the most successful pilot on either side in the Korean War. But I'm going to spring a surprise. The OODA loop will give you only tactical, short-term victory, not strategic victory that will last a long time. In fact, when Boyd initially presented the theory in military circles, he used the example of the German blitzkrieg in World War II. Using light Panzer tanks and a rapidly moving army, the Germans overcame a more formidable French opposition. The Germans may have overrun France quickly in 1940, but we all know who ultimately won the war in 1945.

When I began to contemplate the application of the Vivékin Intelligences Framework to business strategy in fast-moving environments, I was not aware of the OODA loop—incidentally, Boyd never published his work, and his theory is restricted to a set of presentations with overhead slides (briefs) that he made to military audiences. The notion of a cyclical movement in environments of change comes rather intuitively—from cyclonic storms that swirl across satellite weather maps to the feedback loops in adaptive-learning systems, we see how circular movement is characteristic of change. Thus I conceptualized the intelligence-driven strategy process as a cycle of four phases that help formulate strategy—the MAST cycle: mapping, assessing, strategizing, and testing.

THE FOUR PHASES
OF THE MAST CYCLE

Mapping

<u>Function</u>: Chart the landscape; understand the situation.

<u>Questions</u>: What business situations are emerging? Which of the five agilities will I need? In what proportion?

Assessing

<u>Function</u>: Determine my (our) strengths and weaknesses in terms of the five agilities.

<u>Questions</u>: What agilities do we have? What do we need to develop? How strong are we? How weak are we? Which agilities are ready to be used? Which ones need development? How long will it take?

Mapping and assessing will lead to a set of options for action.

Strategizing

<u>Function</u>: Choose the strategy (or set of strategies) that will be best in the long term.

Questions: Which is most appropriate of the several choices for action that the mapping and assessing phases have jointly developed? What are the backup choices? What are the long-term implications of the chosen plan of action? What agilities do we need to develop for the future? What should the scale of the implementation be?

Testing

Function: Deploy the chosen strategy in limited fashion—either in a smaller domain or on a smaller scale—to see the impact of the chosen strategy on the environment.

Questions: How does the chosen strategy work in practice? Are there unforeseen hurdles? Does the implementation create new problems that were not anticipated? Are there new opportunities that were not thought of?

Awareness and Variety of Choices

The key principle that drives an intelligences-oriented strategy is *awareness*. For Sun Tzu, awareness is a precondition for knowledge. Thus chapter 3 of Sun Tzu's *The Art of War* ends with the following conclusion: "It is said that one who knows the enemy and knows himself will not be endangered in a hundred engagements. One who does not know the enemy but knows himself will sometimes be victorious, sometimes meet with defeat. One who knows neither the enemy nor himself will invariably be defeated in every engagement."

Vivéka, the closest word to "intelligence" in Hindu philosophical traditions, comprises two aspects: first, laying out all the possible actions available to us given a situation (awareness); and, second, choosing the best option among those available (discrimination—between right and wrong, good and bad). In Japanese martial arts, the fighter is at his best when he is in *zanshin*, a state of "complete awareness." In *zanshin*, the warrior is constantly alert but also tremendously calm, aware of the things around him, ready for the unexpected to come from any direction. Awareness helps to create a variety of strategic options, and this variety of options creates a position of competitive advantage.

The MAST Cycle in Action

It is very important to understand that I have chosen to discuss MAST as a cycle so that it becomes simple to conceptualize. In practice, however, we do not use a sequential process and always move from one phase to another. In fact, when faced with a real situation or environment, the human brain processes several things at once. In his authoritative book *Strangers to Ourselves: Discovering the Adaptive Unconscious*, Timothy Wilson observes, "The mind is a well-designed system that is able to accomplish a great deal in parallel, by analyzing and thinking about the world outside of awareness while consciously thinking about something else."[81]

Our brain receives and processes about eleven million bits of information every second from our senses and bodies but can consciously process only fifty bits of information per second.[82] So it is mostly unconscious processing, and the subsequent unconscious actions and reactions, that drive the remarkable adaptation of human beings. We unconsciously use the MAST cycle thousands of times every day as we spontaneously sense and respond to situations that emerge in life.

But the word "unconscious" does not imply unmindful—the unconscious processing and spontaneous response are the result of the learning and training that we have gone through from the time that we are born. Some of the adaptive capacity is precoded, genetic—the crystallization of what our species or ancestors learned over millennia—and some of it is what we have personally learned and trained for over the course of our careers and lives. By becoming conscious of the four phases of the MAST cycle, we begin to learn responses to situations so that we form an array of ready and effective responses that we can draw upon when we face a similar situation in the future.

The *mapping* and *assessment* phases operate virtually together and determine which intelligences or agilities are required to solve the problem at hand. The goal of the rapid exchange between the mapping and assessment phases in a single-loop learning mode is to generate multiple solutions to the problem at hand based on the situation's requirements and the availability of appropriate resources. Thus, when the neighbor's kid is at your door at 4:00 a.m. saying, "Mom's having a heart attack, and Dad's traveling," your mapping and assessment phase will yield a bunch of responses: call for an ambulance; do CPR; rush to their house; shout for your spouse. Note that you will think of these responses depending on what resources and capabilities you have available, and also depending on how appropriate the responses are in the situation. Thus, in this case, "give a clot-busting injection" becomes a choice if you are a doctor, but "sing a song" is not a choice, even if you are an award-winning singer. The larger the variety and number of possible solutions that emerge from these interactions during the mapping and assessment phase, the better the strategic agility of the leader or the organization. As is clear, the adaptation in these interactions is governed by a learning process: *What agilities are required? What combination of the agilities we have will work? What other combinations will work?* The learning here is governed by questions of *What?*

The *strategizing* phase takes the set of possible solutions that have emerged from the mapping-assessment interaction and asks deeper questions: Why is one combination better than the other? During this phase one transforms the reactive response to a strategic one by ranking the possible responses in terms of the long-term impact and the breadth of impact they will have. For instance: *Will administering a clot-busting drug have long-term implications on the patient?* or *How will the child at the door be affected by what I do now?* These questions drive the deeper learning that transforms the tactical response into one that is strategic.

The *test* phase is classic in emergent-strategy methodology: We don't know what will work, so we try a small experiment. You are not sure if you should do CPR on your neighbor, so you suggest the option to the 911 operator; depending on the response of the trained operator, you make a decision to do CPR or not. The questions here are deeper: *Does this solution fit with our values? Is this what we want to be remembered for? What will this do for society?* This is much deeper learning that takes the solution beyond our immediate settings and ourselves to the larger world context. After this conceptual overview, let's get more practical in applying MAST.

MAST in Action

The Mapping Phase

Mapping begins with trying to understand the agilities required to meet the challenges of the situation before us or of the environment in which we are operating. In sudden situations, like the neighbor's heart attack, it could call for rapid judgments, and in more mundane settings—planning innovation efforts for the next quarter, for instance—it calls for analysis of environmental trends: competitors' moves, advances in technology, market trends that drive product acceptance.

Below are some questions that might be asked in an

organizational context from the perspective of the five intelligences. You can use these questions to trigger specific and more detailed questions that reflect your company's situation better.

Sample Questions for the Mapping Phase in Organizations

1. Mapping Operational Agility Requirements
   - Service/Platform Flexibility
     - What kinds of scale changes do we anticipate? (Scale)
     - Will we need to be flexible about our product mix? (Variety)
     - Will we have to provide service round the clock? (Time)
   - Time to Market Flexibility
     - Will we need to speed up or extend the time to market during the project?
   - Production Process Flexibility
     - Will we need to change the production process in between?
   - Delivery Channel Flexibility
     - Through what channels will we need to provide service?

- Do customers expect multichannel delivery from the outset or can we offer it in a phased manner?
- Operating Personnel Flexibility
  - Do we anticipate personnel changes in the near future?

2. Mapping Analytical Agility Requirements
- Quality
  - What kinds of changes in quality control should we anticipate?
- Competition
  - Do we foresee any changes in competitive positioning?
- Technology
  - Do we see any disruptive technologies on the horizon?
- Resources
  - What are the chances of there being a scarcity of resources? What about a glut?
- Financial Analysis
  - Will we have to use multiple budget-allocation processes? For example, real options for new technology-driven projects and DCF for traditional business?

- ⋄ Will we see changes in pricing structures? What about costing structures?

3. Mapping Inventive Agility Requirements
   - Product Flexibility
     - ⋄ What kinds of changes do we anticipate in product specifications?
     - ⋄ What kinds of changes will the need to customize bring?
   - Pricing Flexibility
     - ⋄ Will the need to price differentially across market segments call for multiple versions of products or services?
   - Market Flexibility
     - ⋄ Will we see new kinds of demands or new markets that are different from the ones we are targeting? What new products or customizations will they call for?
   - Competitive Flexibility
     - ⋄ Will we have to change designs based on what the competition does?

4. Mapping Communicative Agility Requirements
   - External
     - ⋄ What changes do we anticipate in the ways we reach and persuade customers?

- ❖ Will we need multiple market-survey methodologies?
- ▪ Internal
  - ❖ Will we need new methods of internal communication? New reporting structures?

5. Mapping Visionary Agility Requirements
- ▪ Long-Term Lens
  - ❖ What do we see happening in the long run?
  - ❖ Will this initiative offer short-term or long-term benefit?
- ▪ Wide-Angle Lens
  - ❖ What effect will this initiative have in terms of nature and magnitude of impact on
    - ❖ Customers
    - ❖ Employees
    - ❖ Markets
    - ❖ Our other products and services
    - ❖ Other processes in the organization
    - ❖ Society

The Assessment Phase

While the mapping phase of the MAST cycle provides a perspective on the agilities demanded by the external environment, the assessment phase looks inward to develop an understanding of what resources are available in terms of the five agilities. Thus assessment takes different, even if complementary, paths as it assesses individuals and organizations.

The Individual Perspective

An assessment such as the one available at VIFTest.com will give you your agilities profile (see Figure 2 for a sample).

There are two aspects to your agilities profile: style and inventory. Style determines the individual's natural affinities for using the intelligences/agilities when faced with a situation. In the neighbor's crisis, for instance, what will you do instinctively? Run to their house and perform CPR? Call 911? Call for your wife? Go look up a website for medical advice? One's five agilities style is driven by instinctive adaptation. The assessment tells you which intelligences you tend to rely on instinctively and which ones you don't use as much. As is clear, relying on one agility all the time leads to lopsided responses—the "I have a hammer, so everything looks like a nail" approach. In other words, the style assessment reveals your ability to be sensitive to context.

Let's say the style profile in Figure 2 (the top pentagon) is that of Joe Salesman. What it tells us is that whenever

FIGURE 2. Example of an Individual's Agilities Profile

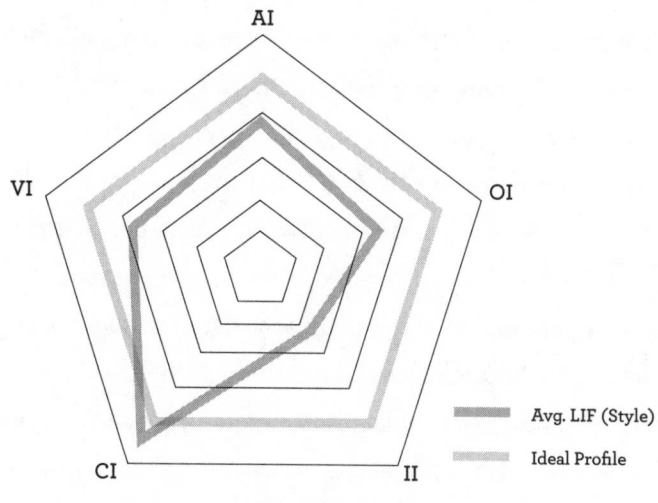

Five Agilities Style

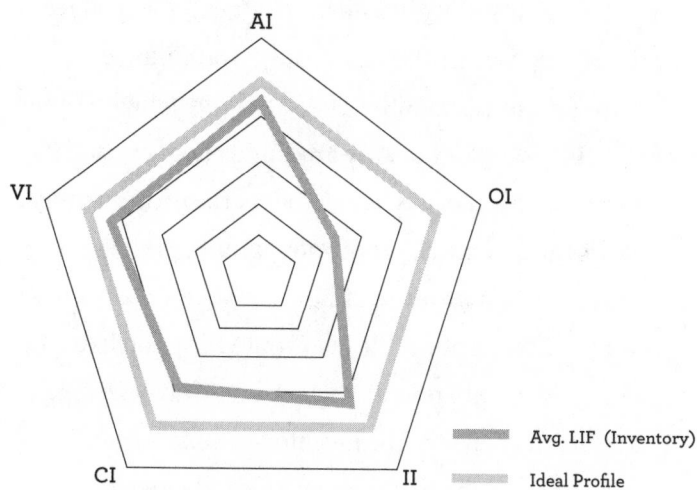

Five Agilities Inventory

Joe is presented with a problem, he tends to rely on his communicative intelligence. As a result, his solutions are all communicatively agile solutions: he may call for a meeting, he may try to resolve things through conversations, he may dash off an e-mail message, and so on. While he is reasonably good at using analytical agility (i.e., adopting different ways of analyzing issues—perhaps he uses different sources of data or employs various analytical methods to slice and dice the data), he does not fare too well with operational and visionary agilities. That is, he does not like to solve problems with a hands-on approach and does not spend much time thinking about long-term impact. The agility that he does not use at all is inventive agility. So when there is a need for new ideas and new approaches, he fares badly. To reinforce what I already said, one's agilities style is about *how* one uses one's agilities. It does not say anything about one's *ability* to be agile. That story is left to the *inventory* assessment, which is the second aspect of your agilities profile.

Inventory is a measure of how adept you really are in each of the five agilities. It tells you which contexts you can be agile in right now and which ones you need to take a backseat in applying. The inventory profile for Joe Salesman is shown in the bottom pentagon in Figure 2. Joe has both good news and bad news in terms of his ability to be multidimensionally agile. His visionary, analytical, and inventive agilities are quite good; however, he has a low score in communicative agility and an even poorer score in operational agility. What this means is that he can handle situations that call for shifting between different types of analysis, situations that call for flexibility in ideation, and even situations that require projections into the future. However, Joe is not the kind of person who can change between different kinds of communication (e.g., if he has been corresponding with a client via e-mail until now, he cannot quickly pick up the phone and have a conversation with the client, even if there is a need to do so). Worse, he cannot change modes of operation—he will fare very poorly if he is asked to move to a new office or work from a client site or adopt a different way of filing sales reports, for instance. Joe can use his inventory assessment to determine what situations he can and cannot be agile in, and seek a suitable position that asks for only the agility challenges he can handle.

If Joe wants to be an agile leader, he will need to work on developing and strengthening the agilities the inventory shows he is weak in. This is where the intelligences-driven approach breaks in a significant way with "personality" tests, which assume a person's personality is fixed—something he or she must learn to live with. Intelligences are like muscles: the more you use them, the stronger they become, and the less you use them, the weaker they become. So you don't have to live with your profile. If you want to develop one or more of the agilities, there are methods you can employ, as we'll see in the next chapter.

Joe Salesman has had several insightful lessons from these two assessments. From the agilities style assessment, he learned not only that he is not being sensitive enough to context in applying his intelligences/agilities, but also which intelligences he is overusing and which ones he is underusing. From the inventory, he learned about his strengths and weaknesses in terms of his agilities, and we have shown him the promise of improving the agilities in which he is weak, so that he can transform himself with practice from Joe Salesman to Joe Leader.

Another significant finding emerges from comparing Joe Salesman's two assessment pentagons. From the agilities style assessment, we can see clearly that Joe relies tremendously on communicative agility in his everyday work; but this contradicts his inventory assessment, which shows he is weak in communicative agility. Clearly, Joe is trying to do something he is not equipped to do. He has a choice: he can live within the limits of his current strengths and weaknesses, or he can work on developing his weaknesses and leveraging his strengths. If he chooses the first, he will have to move to a position that matches his profile—for instance, a position that does not demand communicative agility. If he chooses the second, then he can work on developing both communicative agility and operational agility, and thus move toward becoming an agile leader. Developing a particular agility requires that we put ourselves in simulated situations that make us exercise that agility. In the next chapter, we'll look at samples of such exercises.

Getting back to Joe Salesman, you may rightly ask, Doesn't Joe's agilities style assessment show that he is overexercising his communicative intelligence? With all the work he is giving his communicative agility, why is it not more well developed? The answer is that Joe's communicative agility has not developed because he is using it *out of context*—applying it indiscriminately when it should not be applied at all. To develop, an agility needs to be exercised in an appropriate context. The agilities style assessment shows that Joe lacks *context sensitivity* with communicative agility, and his inventory assessment shows that he lacks communicative agility. So on both counts Joe Salesman needs to work on improving his communicative agility.

The Organizational Perspective

Agility assessment for organizations follows a different method from that used for individuals. The assessment tool takes inputs from various senior executives across the organization, and together they give us an idea of which agilities the company needs and which ones are not important. This assessment by senior executives provides a target pentagon—for example, we see that our company needs operational intelligence, but we don't see much of a need for analytical agility (see Figure 3, for instance).

FIGURE 3. Sample Target Agility Profile: "Discovery" Division in a Pharmaceutical Company

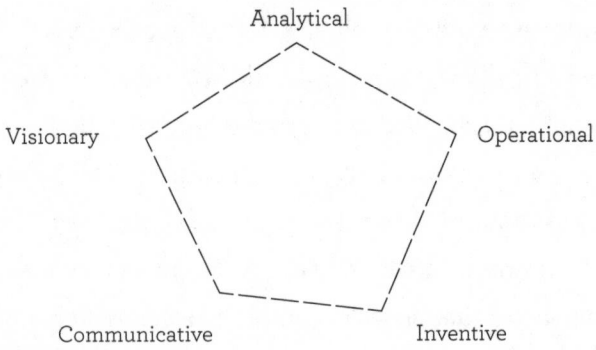

As in the style assessment for individuals, here we assess how the organization recognizes and uses the appropriate agilities in a given context. Again, a group of senior executives who have a good overview of the company provides a 360-degree perspective of how the company reacts to situations. This assessment helps develop the company's agilities style.

FIGURE 4. Sample Organizational Agilities Style: "Discovery" Division in a Pharmaceutical Company

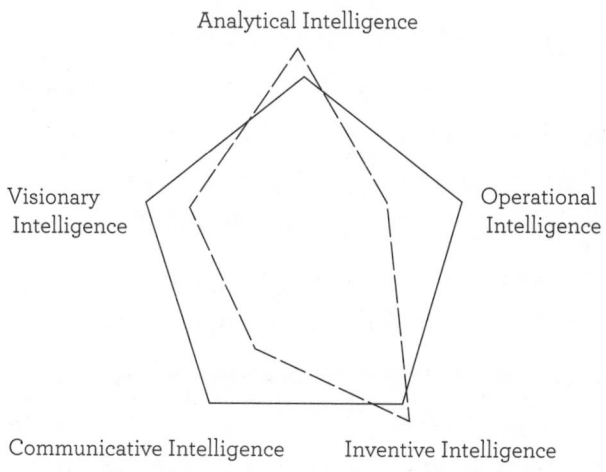

The lopsided pentagon in Figure 4 shows how the Discovery division ("Discovery") is imbalanced in its agilities style. Characteristic of an R&D unit, it overuses analytical and inventive intelligences. While the use of visionary intelligence is in the ballpark range, Discovery underuses operational and communicative intelligences, which is typical of an R&D unit that is far removed from both operations and external-world functions. It may be able to get away with this because it is a business unit within a larger organization, but the misrecognition and misapplication of intelligences can still hurt it in certain circumstances; the division may, for instance, try to respond to an operational problem (such as the processes in drug approval, for example) by trying to generate new processes using its creativity; or, if there is a problem with public relations (e.g., a newspaper report accuses it of unethical conduct in clinical trials), it may tend to spend too much time presenting various analyses of the situation.

An organization's agilities inventory is arrived at through close examination of the various infrastructure technologies, the organization's standard operating policies (SOPs), its design and reporting structure, and of course by ethnographically studying its culture. Without going into the mechanics of how this is done, I show in Figure 5 the agilities inventory assessment for Discovery. Comparing Discovery's agilities style and agilities inventory maps, we see that the Discovery division overuses inventive and analytical intelligences, and underuses operational intelligence.

Ideally, in the strategizing phase of the MAST cycle, the attempt is to find ways to make the organization's agilities inventory as close to a perfect pentagon as possible—since any intelligence may be called upon at any time given the dynamic business environment. However, management may feel that it has a reasonably

FIGURE 5. Sample Organizational Agilities Inventory: "Discovery" Division in a Pharmaceutical Company

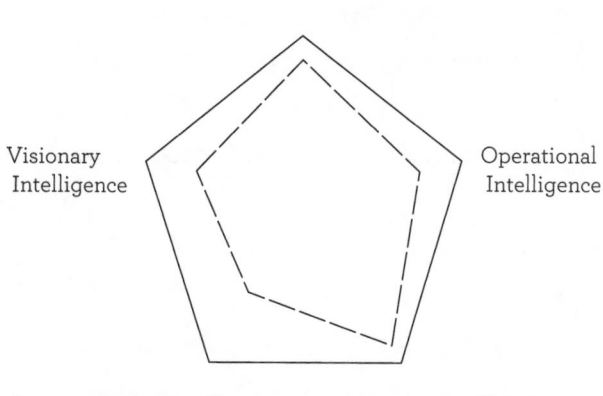

good understanding of the market dynamics in the short- to medium-term period, and may decide on a nonperfect pentagon. Thus, Discovery's target agilities inventory, as shown in Figure 3, is brought to bear.

Given this target agilities profile, the organization's senior executives have to strategize to improve communicative agility in their division and also visionary agility. Workshops to improve individual communication skills, restructuring of communication flows, and perhaps rearrangement of organizational hierarchies and standard operating procedures are some of the methods available to them. Visionary intelligence may be improved by discussing the organization's *values* and whether the business's offerings fit in with those values. Further, comparing the style and inventory profiles, the agilities strategy should also ensure Discovery does not spin its wheels by overanalyzing and inventing, and instead leverages its agility in operations.

A Summary Note

One of the principal concerns about dynamic capabilities, which spills over into discussions of strategic agility, is that we are able to spot companies that have dynamic capabilities only in a retrospective way. In other words, we look at companies that have demonstrated certain agilities and then declare—some may say, in a tautological way—that these companies succeeded because they were strategically agile. The key question is: how do we plan in a forward-looking way so our organization can develop the necessary agilities to succeed in chaotic markets, or so that we, as individuals, can emerge as leaders in the face of rapidly changing and unpredictable circumstances?

We've seen how a company or an individual can use a systematic method that covers four phases of a repeating cycle:

1. *Map* what agilities are required by the changing environment.

2. *Assess* the agilities we possess.

3. *Strategize* around resources (acquiring new resources if necessary) to develop the appropriate agilities needed by the environment.

4. *Test* the strategy before committing to it wholesale.

Just as a fighter pilot in a dogfight continuously executes John Boyd's OODA loop, strategically agile organizations and leaders go through the MAST cycle repeatedly.

We've also seen how to go through the assessment phase of the MAST cycle. While a complete discussion of how to apply the five-intelligences framework is better presented in a separate book, we've seen how we can develop methods to assess the agilities of both an individual and a business entity. Depending on this assessment, we can create a strategy that allows us to develop the mix of agilities that is most appropriate to the operating environment.

FIND YOUR FUNCTIONAL STYLE

Assessment

<u>Directions</u>: For each of the questions below, assign **points (0–10)** to all five choices so that the total for the set is exactly **10** points. Assign **more points** to the choices you feel reflect your company best, and **less or even 0** to the other choices. Do not assign negative points to any choice.

1. When I have to plan a vacation

	Choices	Points
a	I look up various websites or travel books for reviews of vacation spots	
b	I call friends and family for suggestions and opinions	
c	I decide on a place quickly and make the bookings	
d	I consider the implications of the vacation on my finances and my work	
e	I would rather go to a place that is not well-known or well explored	
TOTAL		10

2. If I have missed a flight to an important meeting, I would

	Choices	Points
a	take the first alternate way that occurs to me, since I do not want to waste any time	
b	talk to the people I was going to meet and try to reschedule	
c	explore to see if we can have the meeting electronically, via videoconference	
d	try to understand the impact of my inability to be at the meeting before deciding on my next course of action	
e	determine how much time different ways to reach the meeting place would take	
TOTAL		10

3. If I have to buy a bicycle, a major factor will be

	Choices	Points
a	cost	
b	ride quality	
c	brand	
d	new features	
e	after-sales service	
TOTAL		10

Scoring

ANALYTICAL

1a. _____ 2e. _____ 3a. _____

Total _____

OPERATIONAL

1c. _____ 2a. _____ 3b. _____

Total _____

INVENTIVE

1e. _____ 2c. _____ 3d. _____

Total _____

COMMUNICATIVE

1b. _____ 2b. _____ 3c. _____

Total _____

VISIONARY

1d. _____ 2d. _____ 3e. _____

Total _____

The totals give you a quick idea of how you respond to situations. They tell you which of the five agilities you naturally tend to use given an uncertain situation or problem. The more robust assessment online at VIFTest .com will give you more details about how you use your five intelligences. That assessment will also tell you how strong you are in each of the five agilities, and which ones you need to develop. Most important, the assessment will serve as a tool for introspection, which will set you on the path to become a more nimble leader.

Chapter 9

////////////////////////////////////

Exercises for the Five Agilities

AGILITIES ARE LIKE MUSCLES. You work them, and they become strong; you neglect them, and they become weak. But you're not stuck with your agility profile—you can change it. If you aren't strong in a particular agility, you can develop it with repetition and concerted effort. In this chapter, I will provide some sample exercises for each agility. As you'll see, the exercises to develop into an agile leader are different from those needed to build agilities into your company. And as with physical exercise, once you have a good working understanding of the five agilities, you'll be able to create your own exercises too.

Exercises for Leadership Agilities

These exercises are for you as an individual to develop a particular agility. Remember, when it comes to agility, awareness is key. So keep casting your mind as wide as possible as you search for solutions to the exercises. Before you begin the exercises, have a pencil and a writing pad handy. Writing things down facilitates learning, making new insights easier to grasp and remember. Visit thenimblebook.com for more exercises and exciting follow-ups.

When it comes to agility, awareness is key.

Analytical Agility

There is a debate about whether cheap drugs that violate patent rules should be made available to AIDS patients in Africa.

> "The most fearful thing is hearing that the drugs can't be found—it's like tying a rope round a person's neck," says Charles, a Kenyan man with HIV being treated by Médecins Sans Frontières (MSF). Charles' HIV drug is manufactured in India, which is the source of 80% of

HIV medicines used to treat more than five million people across the developing world. Why? Because in most other countries (particularly developed countries), after a company has designed a new drug, they own the patent for at least 20 years. This means that they are the only company permitted to manufacture it, and so they have control of the price.

The drug industry argues that they need the profits guaranteed by patents to be able to innovate and invest in new drugs. "Patents provide an incentive to the pharmaceutical industry to invest in the development of new medicines," says a statement from the Swiss drug company Novartis. "Without pharmaceutical research and development leading to innovative medicines, poor people will continue to suffer."[83]

Make an argument for both sides of this debate: Why is it justified to provide drugs to terminally ill patients even if the drugs violate patent laws? Why is it wrong to steal the intellectual property that has gone into the discovery of the drug? What facts can you muster for your arguments?

Operational Agility

You decided to work from home today. The kids have already left for school. Your spouse was about to leave for work, and you decided to step out and say good-bye. You have just waved good-bye to your spouse, and as the car goes out of sight, you turn to go inside. You're in your pajamas and are holding a half-full coffee mug. You realize that you're locked out of your home. You can't access your cell phone, because it is locked inside. The neighbors have all left for work. You live in a rural area and no taxis or public buses or trains are available nearby.

Making notes on a sheet of paper, create a plan to enter your house. If some easy solutions pop up ("the back bathroom window is always unlocked," for instance, or "we have spare keys near the air conditioner" or "the newspaper boy is scheduled to come in ten minutes, and I will use his cell phone"), make these unavailable today—the window is jammed, the keys are at the hardware store being duplicated, and it's a newspaper holiday . . .

As you go through the exercise, pay attention to the following:

- What is limiting your operational agility?
    - Are you physically incapable of going through a window?
    - Is it a lack of knowledge—you have a lock pick, but you don't know how to use it?

- ❖ Is it cost—you could break the glass door on the patio, but it costs two thousand dollars?
- ■ What would you need to do to overcome this problem in case it actually did happen?
  - ❖ Leave spare keys somewhere?
  - ❖ Leave an emergency cell phone outside the house?
  - ❖ Have an electronic lock on the door rather than the traditional lock that opens with a key?

Inventive Agility

Rummaging in a box of toys, you have found the following:

- ■ A solar-powered toy motor that works!
- ■ A small flat piece of plastic.
- ■ A three-inch-long thin metal rod.
- ■ Some scraps of colored cloth.

Using only these parts, what toy can you build that might make a child happy?

How many different toys can you imagine making with only these parts?

Communicative Agility

THE SETTING

You are at the airport waiting to board a flight home. It's Friday evening, and you're looking forward to spending the weekend with your kids. You've promised to take them out to the lake tomorrow, and now you remember that as soon as you get home, you must make sure to check the boat. The kids are eagerly looking forward to the outing—you heard the seven-year-old's excitement on the phone as she told you how she'd got all her art supplies ready so she can paint on the excursion.

The insistent ring of your cell phone startles you out of your reverie. Your boss is on the line. An important client can only meet tomorrow. You're the only one he trusts—your presence at the meeting will make the difference between retaining the account or losing it. Can you fly out tomorrow? You curse under your breath as you promise your boss that you will fly out and do what's needed.

THE EXERCISE

The goal of this exercise is to persuade others to see your point of view. Think about how you will persuade your family that you have to postpone the sailing trip. Who will you tell first? Why? Think of each individual and what you will say to him or her. Write down more than one line of argument for each individual. Rank the lines of argument in terms of effectiveness, and justify why you think one will be more effective than the other. What words will you choose? Are there words or references you need to avoid?

Now do the flip side. How would you convince your boss that you need to spend time with your family? Write down at least three lines of argument and rank them: Which line of argument do you think will be most persuasive? Why? Which will be the least convincing?

Visionary Agility

THE SETTING

You notice that the administrative assistant in your office has come in to work with a black eye, and a part of her face is blue. You ask her what happened, and she confides that she is a victim of domestic abuse. You are outraged that this is happening to someone in your office and advise her to separate from her husband. You assure her that your company will do everything to support her, including meeting her legal expenses. She flatly refuses your suggestion, citing family concerns, especially the young children. Moreover, she says, she loves her husband.

THE EXERCISE

Make three lists. Be as specific as you can.

- On one list put down everything you know about her situation.
- On the second, write what you don't know about her situation.
- On the third, list the major issues that you can imagine from her perspective.

Now list the steps you would take to solve the problem.

Examine how your solution can be generalized to address domestic violence issues in society and even across the world.

Exercises for Organizational Agilities

Each of these exercises is best done in a team or across the organization. You can allocate as much time as you wish to each exercise, but I have found that it is not effective to allocate less than thirty minutes to each session. These exercises need not be completed at one time, though if you wish, you could get your team to attend a half-day session in which they exercise all five of their agilities. Also, these are sample exercises to give you a flavor of the types—you could certainly construct your own exercises for follow-up sessions.

Analytical Agility

The table below describes the projected growth of cloud computing.

Research Report on Potential of Cloud Technologies[84]

Application	Potential Economic Impact of Applications in 2030 ($ trillion annually)	Estimated Scope in 2030	Estimated Potential Reach in 2030	Potential Productivity or Value Gains in 2030
Cloud-based Internet	4.2–5.5	2–3 billion more Internet users, most in developing economies	Nearly all Internet applications use cloud as core enabler	$25–85 surplus per user per month
Infrastructure and Operating Expenses	0.5–0.7	$1.5 trillion or 35% of global IT spending in base scenario	Varying levels of cloud adoption across enterprises ▪ All enterprises could have potential to use cloud ▪ Most enterprises may use a hybrid cloud	20–30% productivity gains ▪ Reduced infrastructure and facilities footprint ▪ Higher task standardization and automation
Application Development and Packaged Software	0.3–0.4	$1.7 trillion or 65% of global IT spending in base scenario	▪ Share of public cloud usage may increase as cybersecurity improves	10–15% productivity gains ▪ Standardization of application environment and packages ▪ Faster experimentation and testing

Irrespective of the industry with which your organization is involved, get your team to study this table and write a report on what your organization can do with cloud computing. What potential offerings can your organization make to the market using cloud computing? What internal operations can be changed based on cloud computing? What are the financial implications (both costs and revenues)?

As you do this, make a note of the following:

- How much time your team takes to do this task.
- What blocked analytical agility in your team, and in your organization. (For instance, how easy was it to get the relevant data? Did your team/organization have the ability to do quick analysis? Was your team/organization able to make decisions quickly even with a lack of "complete" information?)
- How you would overcome these blocks. (For instance, do you need to have access to good data sources? Do your team members need to improve their analytical agilities? Does the speed or quality of decision making need to be improved?)
- Did your team try different analytical models? (If they didn't, you could ask them explicitly to do the analysis with other models.)

Operational Agility

Put your team through the following scenario. Pick a critical project in which you are currently engaged as a team. Have members of your team *privately* think of some factors that would create an operational disturbance in this project—for instance, a machine or process breaks down, a supplier announces a delay of several weeks, a collaborator backs out, or a critical resource person resigns. Have the members of your team write these various disruptions on pieces of paper, which they then fold and drop in a bowl. Next, one of you can draw one folded piece of paper to see which operational crisis has hit your team—this adds an element of surprise and fun, and also increases team participation. Give your team thirty minutes to discuss how you would deal with this unanticipated crisis.

After the discussion, here are some of the questions you could have the team discuss:

- What is creating bottlenecks to operational agility?
- Are there single points of failure (SPOFs) that are making your operations inflexible?
- What can you do to remove the bottlenecks and SPOFs?

- In removing existing bottlenecks and SPOFs, are you creating new ones?
- How many alternative ways of overcoming the crisis did your team come up with?
- Can you rank these alternative ways in terms of
  - speed?
  - effectiveness?
  - financial impact?

Make notes from these discussions and circulate them among team members as an action plan to deal with operational emergencies.

Inventive Agility

Have your team pick three or four products or services that your organization now offers. On a big whiteboard, write down the features of these product or service offerings. Then, combining different features from these various products, try to create a new product or service. Make sure the new offering is significantly different from the earlier ones. Pay attention to the following:

- How many new products or services were you able to create? What limited your team from coming up with more options?

- As you considered new offerings, were there any mind-sets that blocked inventive agility?
- Were some options considered outlandish because of a resistance in your team to nontraditional offerings?

You may find it useful to follow up this exercise with the mapping guidelines provided in the section "Mapping Agilities for an Innovation Initiative" that appears later in this chapter.

Communicative Agility

Gather your team and tell them that for the next half hour they will not have access to the Internet or be able to send or receive e-mail. Your team will have to work normally without using e-mail. If possible, this can be done as a real exercise rather than as a paper-and-pen plan in a workshop setting. As your team goes through this exercise, you can draw their attention to the things that make it difficult for them to continue official communication. For instance:

- How much of your work depends on the Internet and e-mail?
- Do you have alternate means of communication if these fail?

- Are your people capable of conducting business on the phone rather than via e-mail?
- Did any previously unused mode of communication come into use? (For instance, that dusty fax machine lying in the corner.)
- Can this new mode become part of standard communication?

Visionary Agility

Ask your team to consider the future of your organization. Working together, develop projections for the future. Some questions you could seek to answer are:

- What will be the growth trends in our industry? What are the implications of these in the long term?
- In what ways is our organization helping the environment?
- In what ways are we harming the environment?
- Will the benefits that we see now last into the future? What conditions need to be met for these benefits to continue? What can disrupt these benefits?
- Are the harmful effects that we see now going to last into the future? What conditions can mitigate these ill effects?

- Will our organization and our products create improvements for society or will they create hierarchies and social division?
- Will our products foster criminal activity? How can they be used to subvert the law?
- Is what we are doing in keeping with our values and long-term vision?
- At the end of every day, do we feel we are doing good to the world?

Mapping Agilities Needed for an Innovation Initiative

Often organizations do not anticipate the flexibilities demanded by a new project or initiative. Sometimes these agilities are required before the initiative is launched (such as a shift in methods to justify investment in the initiative), and sometimes after the launch (sudden scaling up because of tremendous demand for the new product or service). Below is a set of sample questions you could use as a template as your company considers investing in a new initiative. Because the exercise is most effective when it is particularized to your context, it is best that you derive your question set with a group of your executives who have a wide perspective on the organization (perhaps helped by a consultant). Each question addresses a risk factor associated with the organization's agilities. As you discuss the questions and the responses in this group, make sure you keep a running tab of the following:

- What is the probability that the risk factor will come into play? A simple low-medium-high rating or a rank on a scale of 1–5 (1 being lowest and 5 being highest) will suffice.
- What impact will it have if it occurs? Again, a low-medium-high rating or a 1–5 ranking like the one you used in the probability assessment above will suffice. You could also add a little more detail about the impact. For example: Will it be financial? Strategic? Will it affect morale within the organization?
- What assumptions are you making as you estimate the likelihood of the risk factor coming into play and its impact? Are these assumptions valid? Are they time sensitive (change with passing of time)? Under what conditions are they valid?

Analytical Agility

- Have we, or others, tried such an idea before? If so, what were the problems? Identify the problem areas and how they were overcome. Were there successes? What lessons were learned?
- Do we have a database of significant events in the company's history and documentation of successful and failed endeavors?
- Can we partner with some other organization for more knowledge or new technology?
- If we are partnering, what factors affect the knowledge transfer? What is the trade-off?
- What variations could arise in the financial projections (costs and revenues) associated with this new initiative? Consider both direct and indirect impacts.
- Will we need new criteria to determine go/no-go funding for this new initiative?
- How soon would the new project be funded? Will there be sudden funding demands during the project? How can we retain the agility to kill the initiative if it is not doing well?
- How does the new initiative change the risk profile of the organization's project portfolio?
- Is anyone in the market offering such a service/product? If so, how is our idea different from theirs?

Operational Agility

- How much time will we take to move this initiative from prototype to production (time to market)?
- Are we equipped to scale the initiative up or down and be flexible with demand?
- Are we equipped to change the range of the products or the services this initiative is bringing?
- Do we have the ability to cope with lack of resources? Are we capable of substituting resources whenever required?
- Can the project/product serve different customers? If not, what modifications do we need to make?
- Is there scope for idle capacity (bench)?
- How speedily can we implement operational changes?

Inventive Agility

- Will this initiative call for application of knowledge from different domains?
- How much inventiveness will this initiative require once we enter the market?
- Will this initiative create new patents?

Communicative Agility

- Does our advertising need to be different in different markets?
- Do we have multiple channels of communication to reach the outside world? Can we shift seamlessly between these channels?
- Will we create new stories around this initiative? Are we equipped to disseminate these stories through different channels?
- Will the initiative create any controversy? How well is our PR department equipped to handle such controversies?
- Do we see any dangers/opportunities in branding with this initiative? How are we equipped to mitigate the dangers and exploit the opportunities?

Visionary Agility

- What are the long-term effects of the initiative? (Think in specific time frames: one year, two years, five years, for example. Remember that the negative impacts of the Green Revolution in India took several decades to show but were devastating when they materialized.)

- ❖ Social/cultural
- ❖ Environmental
- ❖ Economic
- ❖ Business strategy
- ❖ Technology
- How can gender, age, race, language, disabilities, or cultural differences affect the initiative?
- Who are all the people the initiative will impact, and in what kinds of ways will it impact them?
- What are all the processes the initiative will impact, and in what kinds of ways will it impact them?

Note about the Exercises

As you have seen in this chapter, the intelligences approach is unlike a personality-assessment-based approach. Your agilities profile is not fixed in stone. It is malleable. You can learn new things and new ways, but you can also learn to do old things in new ways. All you need is practice and exercise. And the exercises to build your agilities muscles need not be elaborate or complex. This chapter will have given you some insight into how to build your intelligences, and you can develop your own challenges. In addition, at the thenimblebook.com website, you'll be able to assess your agility mix to see which agilities you're strong in and where you're weak. Starting there, you can practice strengthening your weaker agilities through the many exercises that are available on thenimblebook.com. The website is also a repository of illustrative multimedia examples of how people and companies across the world have used their different intelligences and agilities to solve various kinds of problems. I look forward to seeing you there.

Conclusion

///

THE WINDS OF change—technological shifts, globalized markets, unforgiving and unpredictable competition—are creating volatile, uncertain, complex, and ambiguous (VUCA) environments for businesses. Caught in this maelstrom, companies are struggling to establish business strategies that will ensure success in the long run.

The business response has been to argue that in the face of uncertainty, companies need to be agile. In this book, I've argued that amid increasingly complex change, it is not enough to be agile in one dimension; the failure of companies like Nokia has taught us that we need to be agile in many dimensions. Agility is a short-term, often short-lived tactic, and in order to survive

and thrive in the long term, we need strategic agility—
the ability to be multidimensionally agile and context
sensitive in our application of a combination of agilities.

As we search for models and frameworks to help us
articulate and structure the notion of strategic agility, the
quintessential human quality of intelligence jumps out at
us. Intelligence has driven human agility over millions of
years; it has helped puny humans overcome all kinds of
rough weather and fiery beasts; it has shaped us into what
we are today. Choosing intelligence as the driver of agility
immediately opens up its multidimensional character—
research in psychology has pointed out the immense potential of multiple intelligences. Thus we have a framework
of five intelligences: the Vivékin Intelligences Framework.
And thus, the title of this book, *Nimble*.

The concept of human intelligence brings into sharp
focus what has faded into the background for the past
fifty years in the thinking about management strategy:
the human aspect of business. We realize that in the face
of turbulence, we do not have the luxury of separating
the human from a microeconomic analysis of strategy—
we cannot "know the dancer from the dance." So, the
discussion of strategy morphs into a discussion of leadership, and the intelligences framework shifts seamlessly
between the organizational and the individual.

The first four intelligences in the intelligences framework—analytical, operational, inventive, and communicative—are like the primary colors. Given any situation in the world, agile leaders and companies can generate an appropriate mix of the four intelligences that are needed to lead in that situation. But they need to mix the colors with the medium of the fifth intelligence, visionary intelligence, so that they never lose perspective of the strategic and the wise.

I hope the concepts and examples I've shared will help you become a more dynamic leader, and help your organization weather whatever storms and surprises the future holds.

To get extra materials and continue the experience, scan this code:

A Reward For You

As a reward for having bought and read this book, I'd like to offer you an assessment of your five agilities at a special price. Go to VIFTest.com to get your personal agilities profile using a proprietary online tool that has been developed through years of research.

Acknowledgments

On a dusky summer evening in 1961, a young Indian boarded a Pan Am flight from Boston's Logan Airport with several short stopovers in various places in Europe—he was heading to India. A few hours before he boarded the Pan Am flight, he had defended his thesis on Shakespeare before an examining committee from Harvard University's English department. "Congratulations, Dr. Nagarajan!" the professors had said in the customary greeting that afternoon.

It is not clear whether they knew that he was the first Indian to get his PhD at Harvard, or why he was headed to India after brilliantly completing his degree in a record two years, the time frame allowed by his Fulbright scholarship. What they certainly did not know was that despite offers from universities in the United States to join their faculty, he was going to India to start an English department in a small university in Poona (now Pune).

Decades later, after I became his son-in-law, he told me how he and an office boy had to sweep out a room and carry desks into what became the office of the English department at the University of Pune. "Why did you come back to India when there were so many opportunities in America?" I asked. "There was magic in the air then," he said. Under his leadership, Pune's Department of English became one of India's best.

Dr. Nagarajan's idealism and attention to detail infuse this book—the thinking behind it began in a conversation I had with him one day in early 2000 as we were sipping coffee in our kitchen in Durham, North Carolina. I was then teaching at the University of Minnesota's Carlson School of Management, and my wife Leela was on the faculty of Duke University. We had a somewhat ridiculous 1,400-mile commuting marriage, but both of us loved our jobs, and so continued in our positions. In my research, I had been engaged with the problem of how to understand agility in organizations and how to determine the value of agility in times of uncertainty and unpredictability. "How would we manage situations in which we don't know anything?" Dr. Nagarajan asked. The conversation centered around a discussion of the overlaps between agility and the characteristic human quality of intelligence, and of the concept of intelligence in various philosophical traditions from Greek to Indian. This conversation was the seed of the five agilities framework that I present in this book.

I dedicate this book to the memory of Dr. Nagarajan, who passed away in early 2014. I gratefully acknowledge his inspiring presence in this book and, indeed, in my life.

My wife Leela, an award-winning ethnographer and fellow traveler on our academic journey, has, with her ability to unravel my sometimes convoluted logic, cleared the many cobwebs that clouded my thinking. She has been instrumental in making me understand that we cannot really talk about organizational agility without recognizing the intrinsic value of people and culture. Ethnography, or the art and ethics of engagement, has become a key component of my approach to strategy and an important methodology in my consulting practice.

My professors and colleagues at the Wharton School trained me in the analytic rigor needed to approach business problems—I especially acknowledge Patrick Harker, now president of the Federal Reserve Bank of Philadelphia, for honing my idiosyncrasies in fruitful directions while he directed my dissertation. My colleagues in Information & Decision Sciences (IDS) and in Strategy at the Carlson School at the University of

Minnesota helped me envisage an alternate paradigm for agility through the behavioral lens. My first paper with the intelligences framework was presented at an IDS seminar in 2001, and is still a working paper on the MIS Research Center website. I am especially grateful to Gordon Davis, who graciously shared his insights with a callow assistant professor. My discussions with Andrew Van de Ven proved to be tremendously useful in reworking initial assumptions, and Srilata Zaheer, now dean of the Carlson School, was generous in her feedback, which opened up new avenues of thinking for me. Alok Gupta has been a good friend and scholar who provided much practical advice on things both academic and personal.

My colleagues at Vivékin have helped me hone the intelligences framework into one that can be practically applied in any organization. Our animated discussions have helped clarify several ambiguous academic concepts— understanding the deeper differences between "agility" and "ability," for instance. Thanks to Anitha, Sreedevi, Arvind, and Amit especially for holding my feet to the fire of practice, and for helping to make this book a practical guide for business executives rather than an academic treatise that will gather dust on library bookshelves. They have also been instrumental in refining the Vivékin Intelligences Framework assessment and making it available on the Internet (VIFTest.com). But above all, they have made the writing of this book a pleasure with their insights and warm collegiality.

Several people have helped the earlier incarnation of this book cross two oceans and reach the United States stronger and more polished. My wonderful agent Margret McBride embodies the resilience which *Nimble* advocates. She and her remarkable associate Faye Atchison have been unstinting in their faith in the book and in their support for me. I thank them both deeply. The team at TarcherPerigee: Marian Lizzi, my editor, is an author's dream—savvy, encouraging, and above all, deeply sympathetic. I owe her much. I also thank Lauren Appleton and Brianna Yamashita, who nimbly guided my manuscript into the book you are holding.

Finally, I am also grateful to all the people—from CEOs and heads of business units, to freshly minted software engineers from the United States, India, Europe, and China—who have used *Nimble*'s intelligences-driven method to develop dynamic strategy and resilient leadership. Their encouragement and feedback have helped to make *Nimble*'s framework robust and relevant in turbulent contexts.

Notes

////////////////////////////

1 *Organisational Agility: How Business Can Survive and Thrive in Turbulent Times* (London: Economist Intelligence Unit, 2009). Accessed January 26, 2017: www.emc.com/collateral/leadership /organisational-agility-230309.pdf.

2 Vivékin, the name of my strategy-consulting firm, comes from *vivéka*, the closest Sanskrit word to "intelligence." I elaborate on *vivéka* in chapter 8.

3 Nicholas Burbules and Paul Smeyers, "Wittgenstein, the Practice of Ethics, and Moral Education." Accessed October 1, 2008: faculty.ed.uiuc.edu/burbules/papers/wittethics.html.

4 The EID Parry case is built on the basis of press reports and my interview with Ravindra Singhvi, EID Parry's managing director at that time. I return to this story later in the book.

5 Names have been changed.

6 Hagel, Seely Brown, and Davison argue that the ROA provides insight into how companies leverage capabilities. And agility, of course, is a capability. John Hagel III, John Seely Brown, and Lang Davison, "The Best Way to Measure Company Performance," *Harvard Business Review* blog, March 4, 2010. Accessed June 27, 2017: hbr.org/2010/03/the-best-way-to-measure-compan.

7 *Vivékin* means "the intelligent one" in Sanskrit, and, as mentioned, it is also the name of the strategy consulting company I founded some years ago.

8 Paul Addison, "Why Churchill Lost in 1945," BBC History, 2011. Accessed January 26, 2017: www.bbc.co.uk/history/worldwars /wwtwo/election_01.shtml.

9 Warren Bennis, *On Becoming a Leader* (New York: Basic Books, 2009), xxvi.

10 Lord John Browne, "Lord Goold Memorial Lecture: Marketing Strategy," Speech, Bradford University, London, November 23, 2001.

11 Alan Shepard and Deke Slayton with Jay Barbree, *Moon Shot: The Inside Story of America's Apollo Moon Landings* (New York: Open Road Media, 2011; Kindle edition), Kindle location 3835.

12 Michael Useem, *The Leadership Moment* (New York: Three Rivers Press, 1999), 75.

13 This incident is recounted in part 2 of the three-part article "Apollo 13, We Have a Solution," *IEEE Spectrum* (April 2005). Accessed January 14, 2017: spectrum.ieee.org/aerospace /space-flight/apollo-13-we-have-a-solution-part-2.

14 "Cutting the Cord," *Economist*, October 7, 1999. Accessed January 24, 2017: www.economist.com/node/246152.

15 Edmund L. Andrews, "At&T Completes Deal to Buy McCaw Cellular," *New York Times*, September 20, 1994. Accessed Aug 25, 2017: www.nytimes.com/1994/09/20/business/company-news-at -t-completes-deal-to-buy-mccaw-cellular.html.

16 H. P. Burstyn, "It's AT&T Versus Motorola in Burgeoning Mobile Phone Markets," *Electronic Business* (November 1980).

17 Ian Lerche and John A. MacKay, *Economic Risk in Hydrocarbon Exploration* (New York: Elsevier, 1999), 233.

18 Peter Coy, "Exploiting Uncertainty," *Business Week*, June 7, 1999. Accessed May 14, 2017: www.bloomberg.com/news/articles /1999-06-06/exploiting-uncertainty.

19 Bethany McLean and Peter Elkind, *The Smartest Guys in the Room: The Amazing Rise and Scandalous Fall of Enron* (London: Viking, 2003).

20 The McKinsey-Enron connection has been vividly traced in *The Guardian* (see Jamie Doward, "The Firm That Built the House of Enron," *Observer*, March 24, 2002): www.theguardian.com /business/2002/mar/24/enron.theobserver.

21 McLean and Elkind, *Smartest Guys*, 28.

22 Rhett Butler, "Brazil," Mongbay.com (updated July 13, 2014). Accessed January 15, 2017: rainforests.mongabay.com/20brazil.htm.

23 Scott Wallace, "Last of the Amazon," *National Geographic*, January 2007. Accessed January 15, 2017: environment .nationalgeographic.com/environment/habitats/last-of -amazon.

24 Patrick Manning, "The Slave Trade: The Formal Demography of a Global System," in Joseph E. Inikori and Stanley L. Engerman, eds., *The Atlantic Slave Trade: Effects on Economies, Societies and Peoples in Africa, the Americas, and Europe* (Durham, NC: Duke University Press, 1992), 117–44.

25 Ketzel Levine, "Farming the Amazon with a Machete and Mulch," *Morning Edition*, National Public Radio, February 4, 2008. Accessed January 14, 2017: www.npr.org/templates/story/story .php?storyId=18656632.

26 Marshall Fisher and Ananth Raman, *The New Science of Retailing: How Analytics Are Transforming the Supply Chain and Improving Performance* (Boston: Harvard Business School Press, 2010), 119.

27 Suzy Hansen, "How Zara Grew into the World's Largest Fashion Retailer," *New York Times*, November 9, 2012.

28 Lucy Siegle, "Zara's Way: How Fast Fashion Snared Us with Low Prices, Quick Changes," Ecouterre.com, August 9, 2011: www.ecouterre.com/zaras-way-how-fast-fashion-snared-us-with -low-prices-quick-changes.

29 Compare at YCharts.com: "INDITEX Gross Profit Margin (Quarterly): 56.49% for July 31, 2014" (ycharts.com/companies /IDEXF/ gross_profit_margin) and "Gap Gross Profit Margin (Quarterly): 35.22% for Jan. 31, 2015" (ycharts.com/companies /GPS/gross_profit_margin).

30 Neelam Raajl, "Modi Is Quite Fashionable While Obama Dresses Safe: Tommy Hilfiger," *Times of India*, September 28, 2014. Accessed December 28, 2016: timesofindia.indiatimes.com /home/stoi/all-that-matters/Modi-is-quite-fashionable-while-Obama-dresses-safe-Tommy-Hilfiger/articleshow/43659793 .cms.

31 Hansen, "How Zara Grew."

32 Kasra Ferdows, Michael A. Lewis, and Jose A. D. Machuca, "Rapid-Fire Fulfillment," *Harvard Business Review* (November 2004), 107.

33 Lady [Elizabeth] Hope and William Digby, *General Sir Arthur Cotton, RE KCSI: His Life and Work* (1900; reprint Delhi: Asian Educational Services, 2005).

34 Brett Wallach, *Losing Asia: Modernization and the Culture of Development* (Baltimore and London: Johns Hopkins University Press, 1996), 58.

35 Hope and Digby, *General Sir Arthur Cotton*, 140.

36 Ibid., 40.

37 Much of this story is reconstructed from two articles in the *New York Times*: Amanda Hesser, "A Gift for the Cook, or Carpenter," December 16, 1998, and John T. Edge, "How the Microplane Grater Escaped the Garage," January 11, 2011.

38 Hesser, "A Gift for the Cook, or Carpenter."

39 Gary P. Pisano, "In Defense of Routine Innovation," *Harvard Business Review* blog, June 10, 2014. Accessed May 24, 2017: hbr .org/2014/06/in-defense-of-routine-innovation.

40 George Anders, "How Innovation Can Be Too Much of a Good Thing," *Wall Street Journal*, June 11, 2007.

41 David Robertson, *Brick by Brick: How LEGO Rewrote the Rules of Innovation and Conquered the Global Toy Industry* (New York: Crown Business, 2013), 43.

42 Ibid., 43.

43 General François Amédée Doppet, a former dentist and writer, who commanded French troops in the 1793 Siege of Toulon, is reported to have been repulsed by the sight of blood. He was replaced in three weeks.

44 Robert Forczyk, *Toulon 1793: Napoleon's First Victory* (London: Osprey Publishing, 2004), 59. Gene Klann, *Building Character: Strengthening the Heart of Good Leadership* (San Francisco: Jossey-Bass, 2007), 81.

45 David G. Chandler, *The Campaigns of Napoleon*, vol. 1 (New York: Scribner, 1966), 23–24.

46 Michael Broers, *Napoleon: Soldier of Destiny 1769–1805*, vol. 1 (London: Faber & Faber, 2014).

47 Although Napoléon illustrates communicative agility in this episode, I am reluctant to consider him a model leader—he proved to be an unethical tyrant after becoming emperor.

48 David Livermore, *Leading with Cultural Intelligence: The Real Secret to Success* (New York: Amacom Press, 2010).

49 David Herbert Donald, *We Are Lincoln Men: Abraham Lincoln and His Friends* (New York: Simon & Schuster, 2003), 170.

50 For a detailed analysis of the communicative and branding implications of Gandhi's Salt March see Suchitra, "What Moves

Masses: Dandi March as Communication Strategy," *Economic & Political Weekly* 30, 14 (April 8, 1995), 743–46.

51 Rajmohan Gandhi, *Gandhi: The Man, His People, and the Empire* (Berkeley: University of California Press, 2008), 303. Here is an example of how disruptive innovation builds on incremental innovation: Gandhi had actually been thinking about salt for many years before his "flash" recognition of the potential of the salt satyagraha. In 1891—nearly forty years before—as a student in London, he had written about the salt tax; he had subsequently discussed it in his book *Hind Swaraj* (1909), and he had referred to it many times before 1930.

52 Ibid., 303.

53 Ibid., 308.

54 It helped that taxes had figured centrally in America's fight for independence from the British; the French Revolution too had been galvanized by a resistance to a salt tax in particular.

55 Gandhi, *Gandhi*, 308.

56 On April 13, 1919, in Jallianwala Bagh, a public square in Amritsar, Punjab, British troops led by General Reginald Dyer fired nonstop for ten minutes at an unarmed crowd that had assembled in nonviolent defiance of a curfew order. The Indian National Congress estimated that about one thousand men, women, and children were killed, and about six hundred injured. The British figures were, of course, remarkably lower.

57 Bernard Imhasly, *Goodbye to Gandhi? Travels in the New India* (New Delhi: Penguin Books India, 2007), xviii.

58 Michael Dobbs, "Rudy's 'Spontaneous' Cell Phone 'Stunt,'" *Washington Post* blog, October 8, 2007. Accessed June 27, 2017: voices.washingtonpost.com/fact-checker/2007/10/let_rudy_be _rudy.html.

59 Doris Kearns Goodwin, *Team of Rivals: The Political Genius of Abraham Lincoln* (New York: Simon & Schuster, 2005).

60 Melinda Beck, Sylvester Monroe, and Linda Prout, "The Tylenol Scare," *Newsweek*, October 11, 1982, 32.

61 Recounted in "Crisis Communication Strategies," US Department of Defense. Accessed on January 25, 2017: www.ou.edu /deptcomm/dodjcc/groups/02C2/Johnson%20&%20Johnson.htm.

62 Susan Tifft and Lee Griggs, "Poison Madness in the Midwest," *Time*, October 11, 1982, 24–25.

63 "Deadly Combination: Ford, Firestone and Florida," *St. Petersburg Times*, May 29, 2001.

64 John Greenwald, "Inside the Ford/Firestone Fight," *Time*, May 29, 2001. Accessed June 1, 2017: content.time.com/time/business /article/0,8599,128198,00.html.

65 Bari Weiss, "Groupon's $6 Billion Gambler," *Wall Street Journal*, December 20, 2010.

66 Robert Cialdini, "The Power of Persuasion," *Stanford Social Innovation Review* (Summer 2003), 18–27.

67 Jonah Berger, *Contagious: Why Things Catch On* (New York: Simon & Schuster, 2013).

68 Shira Ovide, "Groupon IPO: Growth Rate Is 2,241%," *Wall Street Journal* blog, June 2, 2011. Accessed June 27, 2017: blogs.wsj .com/deals/2011/06/02/groupon-ipo-growth-rate-is-2241/.

69 Jack Kroll, "A Magnificent Life of Gandhi," *Newsweek*, December 13, 1982, 60.

70 Conversation with C. Rajagopalachari, September 1, 1947, in *Collected Works of Mahatma Gandhi*, vol. 96, 319. Accessed June 27, 2017: http://www.gandhiashramsevagram.org/gandhi -literature/mahatma-gandhi-collected-works-volume-96.pdf.

71 John Briley, *Gandhi: The Screenplay* (London: Duckworth, 1982).

72 Patrick Barta, "Feeding Billions, a Grain at a Time," *Wall Street Journal*, July 28, 2007.

73 Kenneth R. Weiss, "In India, Agriculture's Green Revolution Dries Up," *Los Angeles Times*, July 22, 2012.

74 Jim Stengel, *Grow: How Ideals Power Growth and Profit at the World's Greatest Companies* (New York: Crown Business, 2011).

75 Beth Ritter, "Why Live the Greater Good?" Burt's Bees, 2010. Accessed January 29, 2017: www.capital.org/eweb/upload/CAI /cai-main/public/2010/2010-02-25c_burts_bees.pdf.

76 Louise Story, "Can Burt's Bees Turn Clorox Green?" *New York Times*, January 6, 2008.

77 Personal conversation with a then senior executive of Burt's Bees who is now no longer with the company.

78 Deanna Utroske, "Burt's Bee's Gets Credit for Category Growth at Clorox," CosmeticsDesign.com, February 7, 2017: www .cosmeticsdesign.com/Business-Financial/personal-care-brand -Burt-s-Bees-gets-credit-for-Clorox-category-growth.

79 "Fiorina Left Out in Cold after HP Failure," ITP.net, February 20, 2005. Accessed June 27, 2017: www.itp.net/491269-fiorina-left -out-in-cold-after-hp-failure/?tab=article.

80 Frans Osinga, *Science, Strategy and War: The Strategic Theory of John Boyd* (New York: Routledge, 2007).

81 Timothy Wilson, *Strangers to Ourselves: Discovering the Adaptive Unconscious* (Cambridge, MA: Harvard University Press, 2002), 8.

82 George Markowsky, "Information Theory," *Encyclopædia Britannica* online. Accessed June 27, 2017: www.britannica.com /EBchecked/topic/287907/information-theory/214958/Physiology.

83 "The Great Patent Debate," Medscape.com. Accessed June 12, 2017: www.medscape.com/viewarticle/775186_2.

84 Adapted from a McKinsey Global Institute Research Report.

Index